W9-CBZ-594

SAINT NICHOLAS:
LIFE AND LEGEND

HARPER & ROW, PUBLISHERS
New York, Evanston, San Francisco, London

Saint Nicholas. Icon at Mount Athos, Greece. *Nicholas Tombazi, Psychico-Athens*

SAINT NICHOLAS:
LIFE AND LEGEND

MARTIN EBON

FIRST EDITION

Designed by Gloria Adelson

Library of Congress Cataloging in Publication Data

Ebon, Martin.
  Saint Nicholas: life and legend.
  Bibliography: p.
  1. Nicholas, Saint, Bp. of Myra. 2. Santa Claus.
BX4700.N55E26 1975   282'.092'4 [B]   75–9329
ISBN 0–06–062113–3

75 76 77 78 79 10 9 8 7 6 5 4 3 2 1

To John A. Nalley (1917–1971), friend and colleague, with whom I shared my first ideas about this book

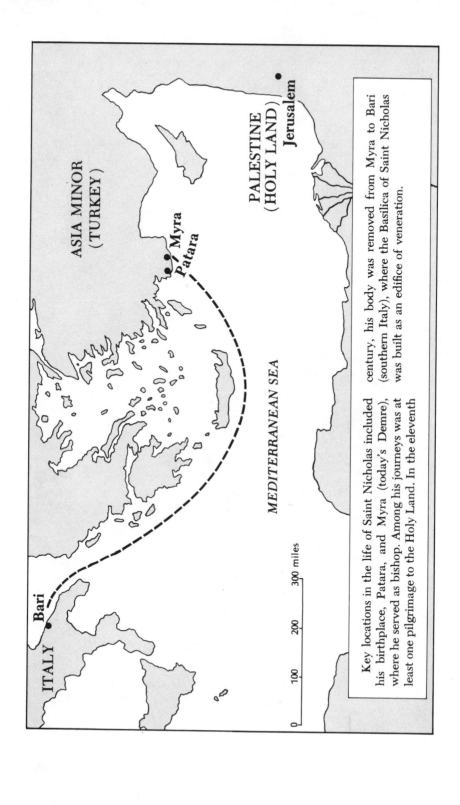

Key locations in the life of Saint Nicholas included his birthplace, Patara, and Myra (today's Demre), where he served as bishop. Among his journeys was at least one pilgrimage to the Holy Land. In the eleventh century, his body was removed from Myra to Bari (southern Italy), where the Basilica of Saint Nicholas was built as an edifice of veneration.

CONTENTS

1. HOW DID SAINT NICHOLAS BECOME SANTA CLAUS?

When Nicholas was born, in Patara, he was said to be such an unusual infant that he was able to stand up in his bath. This painting, from the Studio of Luca Signorelli, is entitled "The Birth of Saint Nicholas of Bari," making the baby's physical precosity retroactive to his birth. *The High Museum, Atlanta. Gift of the Samuel H. Kress Foundation, 1958*

Once there was a Saint Nicholas, an awe-inspiring patron of all seafaring men, whose fame spread from the Eastern Mediterranean to the Western world and whose very name inspired pious devotion and trust in Christian society. Today, we are familiar with the red-coated figure of Santa Claus, whose face greets us from store windows and television screens at Christmastime and who is said to come down a chimney to leave Christmas presents for boys and girls.

Saint Nicholas and Santa Claus are the same. With the evolution of the name has come, through the centuries, a changed image: the revered saint is now a jolly friend of children. Typical of the older image are stories of his miraculous deeds. According to one legend, the saint was traveling on a ship to the Holy Land when he dreamed that a fierce storm would endanger the boat. He warned the crew of the coming danger, but assured them that it would pass. When a storm actually broke out, one of the sailors fell to his death from a mast. But, once the high wind subsided, Saint Nicholas restored him to life.

By contrast, during the Yuletide Santa Claus sits on a somewhat elevated armchair in the toy section of a department store. He is genial, laughs a good deal, asks each child whether he or she has been "good or bad," and listens to hundreds of hesitant or bold requests for toys or other Christmas gifts. When the presents are opened on Christmas morning, small children's pleasure is heightend by the idea that Santa Claus has fulfilled their wishes and brought them a sackful of gifts.

What links the Byzantine saint, best known as the patron of sailors, and the white-bearded, portly figure we know so well? How, across sixteen centuries, did we happen to inherit the Saint Nicholas traditions in our own specific way?

The stories and legends of his life and miracles tell us much about earlier generations who looked up to Saint Nicholas, just as today's Santa Claus tells us a good deal about ourselves. The changing image depended greatly on the eyes of the beholder. Imagine that you are looking up into the clouds on a December evening. One cloud formation, for a brief moment while touched with red by the sinking sun, looks just like a kindly old man with a white beard. But when the wind shifts, the image changes. He is no longer plump and smiling but lean and serious. Next, he seems remote, elusive, mystical. And finally he looks once again protective, benign, and approving.

In just this way, mankind's image of Saint Nicholas has changed through the ages. For hundreds of years, the saint has been a figure in religion and folklore that reflected the needs and hopes of millions of men, women, and children. He has been many things to many people. Although Saint Nicholas has been associated with children from the very beginning, he has also been—and in many places remains—the patron saint of seafaring men, of merchants, of marriageable young women, of the falsely accused, of endangered travelers, of farmers, and even of pawnbrokers.

Saint Nicholas, the most human of saints, was always ready to help where need existed. His protective powers enabled him to save sailors from being shipwrecked. He miraculously multiplied a shipment of grain to avert famine. He liberated falsely accused men on the eve of their executions. He brought three students back from the dead. He exposed a fraudulent debtor, bested pagan gods, exorcized demons.

By his very humanity, the saint reflected popular hopes and fears. He changed because human needs changed. He is what he is today, as Santa Claus, because we yearn for a season of altruism, childlike innocence, and "Peace on Earth." We look for the visitation of a kindly, familiar figure who makes children of us all.

Human needs today are different from those of the early period of Christianity as it emerged from Roman persecution, from the ferment and groping of the Middle Ages, and from the twelfth century that brought the Saint Nicholas cult to its peak. At one time, the saint stood third, behind Jesus and the Virgin Mary, in frequency and intensity of worship; this was particularly true in Russia. Hundreds of churches were dedicated to him. Nicholas became a popular name for boys and, in such adaptations as Nicole, for girls.

When the Protestant Reformation swept parts of Europe, efforts were made to eliminate the Nicholas cult. But something stronger than theological argument resisted these pressures: a deep human need to retain the image of the most human of saints. Today, all of Christianity, and much of the non-Christian world, accepts the saint's heritage and its many expressions. Excessive commercialization of Santa Claus may irritate us, but we should remember that the hurly-burly of a modern Christmas is simply a contemporary version of traditional church fairs, with their bazaars, fun rides, and games of chance. We are, as these things go, no better and no worse than those before us.

Many sincere voices are raised today against nonreligious aspects of the Santa Claus symbol. Much of this criticism is valid; yet we are heirs to a civilization in which the secular and the religious were closely linked. Greece, to whose culture the Saint Nicholas cult originally belonged before it spread throughout the world, is to this day a society in which both elements are intertwined. Elsewhere, a ship may be launched with a bottle of champagne; in Greece, that nation of sailors, it is more likely to be blessed by a priest who invokes the name of Saint Nicholas. The Greek tradition spread into Russia through the Ukraine, and to western Europe through southern Italy. And, as we shall see, in the United States today's universal Santa Claus image took on definitive form.

Saint Nicholas has thus been an image basic to human aspirations, be they religious, secular, or both. Indeed, in today's effort to revive religious vitality, the saint's figure seems well suited to the task of deepening such interests. That need not mean a return to earlier, literal requests and prayers for intercession or miracle, but it might well mean a new infusion of ethical and mystical elements into a materialistic life-pattern.

It is odd that we find it so difficult to think in abstractions, even on such themes as altruism. No matter how strongly we feel about something, at least one of our five senses needs to be stimulated: a stained-glass window, the smell of incense, the taste of wine, the sound of a hymn, the touch of something as familiar as a book of prayer.

But more than anything else, we need a human or superhuman example. The child who is named after a saint is urged, at least unconsciously, to live up to the name, to live in the spirit of the saint, to imitate, emulate, or at least not to disgrace the example. And the characteristics of this example are best illustrated by anecdote. For this reason, the stories of Saint Nicholas's miraculous intervention have served, first of all, as moral guidance. Next, they were obviously told and written down for their dramatic content. Artists have contributed to this drama with paintings which, in many cases, sharpened the elements of conflict and solution.

As we read these stories, it is well to remember that legends of heroes, saints, and villains were literary forerunners of the short story and the novel. Epics, stories of miracles, of witchcraft, of battles against visible and invisible antagonists were the products of artistic imagination, however pious, which today have their equivalents in the theater, the motion picture, and the television drama. Several dramatic events connected with Saint Nicholas were made into miracle plays in the twelfth and thirteenth centuries; performed in churchyards or in public squares, their narratives and personalities held the attention of popular audiences.

How much, then, is life and how much legend when we speak of Saint Nicholas? Actual biographic data on the saint is severely limited. Moreover, the core of facts has tended to be enveloped by pious fantasy as century followed century. Although the saint lived in the fourth century, the supposed records of his life and miracles—at least those that have remained intact—only began to accumulate many centuries later. To what degree these are based on earlier writings or oral traditions is hardly ever clear. The various *Vitae,* or "life stories," of the saint borrow heavily from each other. Perhaps the earliest is the *Vita Per Metaphrasten,* which contained five major miracle stories, which are repeated and somewhat amplified in the *Vita Per Michaelem;* the most comprehensive, the *Vita Compilata,* sought to include all known facts on Saint Nicholas and contains data, such as the names of his parents, not recorded elsewhere.

The life of Saint Nicholas is a reflection of European and American cultural evolution. The role played by fairly recent American writers in the development of the now well-known Santa Claus personality is much greater than is generally assumed. The cultural give-and-take between the Old World and the New has also shaped and colored the Santa Claus image to the point where a Greek magazine will today publish, at Christmastime, a colorful picture of a typical "American" Santa Claus on its cover—beard, red suit, and all. The symbol of Saint Nicholas thus completes its round trip, from Byzantine to modern Athens, over a period of sixteen centuries.

How did it happen? How did the pious miracle worker, Saint Nicholas of Myra and Bari, become the legendary figure who visits homes through a chimney on Christmas Eve? How did the forbidding figure of Byzantine icons become "the jolly old elf" of the present day? Where did he get his red coat? The white beard? The reindeer? How did the patron saint of sailors grow into a gift-giver for children, who knows whether they were "naughty or nice"?

It is quite a story!

This painting, in the possession of the Uffizi in Florence, is attributed to Titian. It shows Saint Nicholas with mitre, holding what is presumably a volume of Holy Scripture, the three symbolic balls resting on the book. *Alinari*

Icon of Saint Nicholas at Mount Athos, the Greek monastery. According to legend, this mosaic had been submerged in the sea for 300 years. When it was recovered by fishermen, mussels had fastened themselves to the upper section of the saint's forehead; as these were removed, the icon bled. *Nicholas Tombazi, Psychico-Athens*

2. YOUNG NICHOLAS
OF PATARA

A fourteenth-century painting showing the saint as he throws a bag of gold coins through the window to help the dowryless girls. This fresco was done by an artist of the Veronese School and is part of the collection at San Zeno Maggiore, Verona. *Frick Art Reference Library, New York*

Nicholas was born in Patara, possibly in the year 280. Today, the town of Patara is located in Turkey, not far from Myra (now Demre), where Nicholas later gained fame as a bishop. Both small towns are near the coast of the eastern Mediterranean. According to the *Vita Compilata*, the boy's parents were well to do, apparently from an inheritance. They were naturally pious people "who did not have to go in for such dramatic proof of their faith as walking barefoot on hot tar or holding it in their hands." This means that they did not practice firewalking, an ancient rite still found in India and the Fiji Islands. Firewalking is still practiced annually in northern Greece on May 21, the name day of Saint Helen and Saint Constantine.

Little Nicholas is credited with precocious religiosity, even in babyhood. He did not demand his mother's breast on fast days, Wednesday and Friday, except after sunset. The record of his birth compares Nicholas with a biblical figure, Samuel, whose mother had been sterile until his conception; Nonna, Nicholas's mother, had no children until she gave birth to him. In the First Book of Samuel, in the Old Testament, Hannah, wife of Elkanah, "prayed unto the Lord," who had "shut up her womb." She asked God to let her give birth to a boy, and she "vowed a vow" that he would devote his life to divine worship. She said, "Remember me, and not forget thine handmaid, but wilt give unto thine handmaid a man child, then I will give him unto the Lord all the days of his life" (1 Sam. 1:11). The biblical Samuel was precocious in his worship and was "in favour both with the Lord and also with men" (1 Sam. 2:26). Baby Nicholas not only showed his piety by observing the fast days, he was a sturdy child who managed to stand up prematurely in his wash basin and crib.

Saint Simeon the Translator (Metaphrastes) writes that young Nicholas "showed from the beginning that he wanted to please God." He was a good student, attended church services regularly, where "he assisted the older men, so that he might benefit from their example and guidance." His father's name may have been Epiphanius, and the family was well established in the community. The parents, "devoted Christians," were "not so poor as to be scorned by others, but neither so rich as to be boastful; they had enough to support themselves and still give to the poor."

Later religious historians appear to have drawn events from the life of Nicholas's uncle, whose name he shared, into the saint's own life story. His father's brother served as bishop in a neighboring community where young Nicholas often visited and helped with church services. Under Uncle Nicholas's tutelage, the young man learned the texts of prayers, details of rituals, and showed a remarkably quick mind and sincere devotion.

Saint Simeon writes that, "being a person of quality, having won wide respect and now having grown into manhood in mind as well as body," young Nicholas was ordained into the priesthood when he was nineteen years old. His uncle the bishop, addressing him as he took his vows, prophesied that his nephew would offer guidance and consolation to many, would himself attain the rank of bishop, and "live a life of enlightenment." This account adds:

"From the minute the saint became a priest, one can hardly keep count of the virtue and goodness he spread about him, of the nights spent at his devotions, days of fasting, steadfast good will, and his prayers for all. Observing this, his Uncle, the Bishop Nicholas, found the young man's eagerness admirable. And when he went on a pilgrimage to Jerusalem, the Bishop left Nicholas as his deputy, to oversee the monastery he had built, and which he had called New Zion. The saint administered both the Bishopric and the Monastery as competently as if he had been the Bishop himself."

Even before he became a priest, young Nicholas engaged in a deed of generosity which, in its symbolism, marked his life in a characteristic way. From this act, which involved gifts for three girls, or young women, may have grown the gift-giving tradition with which Saint Nicholas's name has since become so strongly linked. As the story is told by various sources, a widowed nobleman lived in the same town as Nicholas and his parents. Once well to do, but now penniless and desperate, the man found himself unable to take care of his three teenage daughters.

Nicholas heard that the distraught father had decided to "sell off" his oldest daughter, presumably into slavery or prostitution. To forestall this, but not give himself away, Nicholas tied three hundred florins into a handkerchief. After dark, he sidled up to the house of the distraught father and threw the money through an open window. This act has been dramatized in many paintings, particularly in twelfth-century Italy, as well as in sculptures, woodcuts, and stained-glass windows.

With the first daughter saved, the household managed to survive for a time. But quite soon the father was in financial straits once more. Before anything untoward could happen, however, Nicholas did the good deed all over again. Naturally, the father was pleased and puzzled. When the third daughter was in danger and the money once more came flying through the window, her father caught Nicholas in the act, thanked and praised him, and the secret was a secret no longer. In all three cases, the father had been able to use the money as a dowry, so all three girls could be married.

Simeon Metaphrastes writes that Nicholas had just thrown the third money gift quickly into the window when he realized that the father had spotted him. Nicholas tried to get away quickly, but the father caught up with him. The father told Nicholas, "If you had not saved us in time, our family would have been destroyed, materially and morally."

Nicholas was embarrassed. He asked the father, "Please, do not tell anyone of this deed as long as I live; I hold you responsible, in the presence of God, to keep my secret safe." Only after the death of Saint Nicholas did the father reveal the generous action Nicholas had taken as a young man. Simeon saw in the gifts to the three girls a pattern of Nicholas's later life. He wrote: "Now that we know of this one deed, we are able to understand the other achievements he tried to keep secret, seeking to avoid the praise of men and hoping only for God's approval. Yet, the more he tried to hide his qualities, the more did God reveal his true nature, in order to honor him, just as he had honored God through his deeds of mercy."

This incident has come down to us without much embellishment by later biographers. It is the story of a simple, spontaneous good deed; it lacks the grandeur of the supernatural found in most other anecdotes concerning Saint Nicholas's acts on earth and, after his bodily death, through appearances as a saintly apparition endowed with miraculous powers. Such divine gifts are implied in one event that is said to have taken place during Nicholas's pilgrimage to Jerusalem.

Following the example of his uncle the bishop, Nicholas wanted to visit the holy centers of Christianity. To prepare himself for this visit in an atmosphere of serenity, Nicholas decided to travel on an Egyptian boat where no one knew him. Other pilgrims were also making the same journey. During the first night of the trip Nicholas dreamed that the Devil was cutting the ropes that held the ship's main mast. He interpreted this to mean that the boat would run into a severe storm. In the morning he told the sailors of this vision, warned that there was trouble ahead, but also reassured them: "Don't be afraid. Trust in God because he will protect you from death."

Nicholas had hardly finished speaking when dark storm clouds covered the sky. The sea around the sailing ship quickly became turbulent. Although they were close to the coast, wind and water grew so violent that it was impossible to steer the boat into calmer waters. Captain and crew lost control of the ship. They pulled down all sails, but the wind continued to batter the boat unmercifully.

The sailors were frightened to death, literally in fear of perishing. They begged Nicholas to pray that they might escape unharmed. One sailor climbed the main mast to tighten the ropes, as the mast threatened to crash across the ship. Having finished his dangerous task, and while climbing down, the sailor lost his footing. He fell to the deck and was killed.

Meanwhile, following the saint's prayers, the storm subsided, and the crew began to breathe freely. But their relief and gratitude were muted by the fate of the fellow sailor whose lifeless body had been taken below. Nicholas, hoping to wipe out the memory of their trial completely, prayed for the dead sailor. Quickly, and miraculously, the man was revived "as if he had only been asleep, and awakened without any pain whatever."

This set a pattern for healing for Nicholas. Crew members and passengers were full of awe and praise for him. When the boat reached port, and before Nicholas could continue his journey to Jerusalem by land, he was approached by many sick people who asked him to pray for their recovery. He was able to restore all of them to health. After stopping in port for one day, Nicholas continued his journey to the Holy Land.

Although it is possible that Nicholas visited Palestine more than once, this is the only account of a journey to Jerusalem that has come down to us in the literature. He visited the Holy Sepulchre, Golgotha, and several other holy sites. Simeon tells us that Nicholas had planned to stay in the Holy Land for several weeks, but "an angel of the Lord ordered him" to return home immediately. This implies that Nicholas was being prepared to act in yet another miraculous manner and also that there was an emergency in his home parish.

At the port, trying to find a boat in a hurry, Nicholas went from ship to ship asking to be taken back quickly. One boat was just being loaded, and the captain said, "We will go wherever our fare asks us to go." Nicholas answered that he would pay "to be taken directly to Patara in Lycia." Captain and crew, however, tried to mislead the saint because they wanted to stop over at their own home port on the way.

There was a fair wind, and they set sail, but not directly toward Patara. God, Simeon writes, "did not want to have the Saint suffer any delay or disappointment," and so he "raised a violent storm that caused the ship's rudder to be damaged beyond repair." As a result, the boat drifted rudderless across the sea, at the mercy of every wave and every gust of wind. The sailors feared that they would either perish in the storm or just drift until they died from lack of food and water.

But, with the sea calmed by divine intervention, the boat began to drift quite purposefully in a specific direction. On and on for many miles it moved. At last, they saw land, and the ship moved close to port. Captain and crew were awed to discover that the ship, far from drifting aimlessly, had taken them directly to Patara where Nicholas had wanted them to go in the first place. Overwhelmed by the dual miracle of their own survival and the safe arrival at Saint Nicholas's destination, they asked his forgiveness. He told them kindly but firmly, "From now on, don't try to fool anyone." Then he asked them to repair their ship's rudder, be on their way, and have a good journey home.

Simeon ends his account of this eventful pilgrimage as follows:

"And thus the Saint returned to his homeland. I cannot tell you with what joy his fellow countrymen greeted him, how pleased they were to see him again. Young and old, men and women, everyone came to meet him. Among them were the

monks of the monastery of New Zion which his uncle had earlier let him administer. The Saint met them, speaking the words
of the Lord and teaching the way of salvation for Christian
souls.

"In this manner, the Saint was respected and loved by all. As
people observed his goodness, many followed his example and
teachings. They scorned a material, transient existence and
placed their trust in the eternal. Being humble, the Saint sought
to avoid men's praise, but once again he could not hide his
virtues, as they were God-given and served all those who followed his guidance."

The pilgrimage, the miraculous events on the two sea journeys, and the welcome Nicholas received upon returning
home, marked the end of his young manhood. Soon he would
become a bishop of Myra. On the eve of Saint Nicholas's ap-
pointment, witnesses claimed, Jesus appeared to Nicholas and
gave him a copy of the Scriptures while the Holy Mother
handed him a stole. Thus, the *Vita Compilata* relates, "Nicholas
had been selected by the Lords and subsequently was appointed Bishop of Myra."

The stories of his interventions on the two sailing ships were
the basis of Saint Nicholas's role as patron saint of sailors. This
has remained the case, to this day, in the Eastern churches
where his role as a gift-giver for children has either been nonex-
istent or a recent exotic import from the West.

Another miraculous rescue of sailors is attributed to Nicholas
when he was a few years older and already Bishop of Myra.
Since it parallels the other two stories, it is cited here as it comes
down to us from the *Vita Per Michaelem*. According to this
source, a ship in the eastern Mediterranean ran into severe
difficulties. Apparently, the boat was battered by wind and water, ran aground in shallow coastal waters, and the crew was
unable to move it into deeper channels.

Having heard of Saint Nicholas's power, captain and crew
prayed that he might help them, even from a distance. They
had never met him, but his fame had reached them, and they
believed that his prayer and intervention might save them and
their ship. As they told the story later, the saint himself actually
appeared on the ship. His appearance was so real that he had
a physical presence and displayed physical strength; in fact, his
apparition seemed to have superhuman strength.

Rather than restricting himself to prayers and urgings, the saint gave them a strong and skillful helping hand. He helped them to retie and strengthen ropes holding the masts, and he worked by their side as they used poles to force the ship out of shallow waters and off the rocks that endangered the ship. If the boat had remained stranded, the waves would have battered it into a wreck. But with the saint's participation the boat was freed, remained undamaged, and was able to set sail for the coast. As soon as the boat was out of danger, the materialized apparition of Nicholas disappeared as suddenly as it had appeared.

The ship took refuge in a cove, and the sailors went ashore looking for a church to thank God for their good fortune. As it happened, their journey took them to Myra. They encountered many priests, but suddenly they recognized the saint himself from the apparition they had seen on the boat. Doubly awed, the sailors threw themselves at his feet and asked him how he had managed to hear their prayers and urgings. He answered that a life devoted to the divine permits a man to be so clear-sighted as to be able, as in this case, actually to see others in danger and hear their calls for help. He urged them to devote their own lives to pious service to God.

The historical Saint Nicholas, to the degree that we can see his actual life in retrospect, reached religious maturity at an early age. From his legendary childhood self-deprivation to acts of generosity in his years as a young man, then on through his pilgrimage to the Holy Land and the miracles at sea, Nicholas passed into mature years of service as a dignitary of the church.

When Nicholas secretly threw a bag of gold through the window of an impoverished nobleman so that one of his daughters would have a dowry, he was said to be still a young man and not even Bishop of Myra. This painting of "Saint Nicholas Providing Dowries," by Lorenzo di Bicci (1373–1452), shows him quite mature and with a halo. The painting is a panel from the predella of an altarpiece completed in 1433 for the monastery of San Niccolò in Florence. *The Metropolitan Museum of Art, New York. Gift of Coudert Brothers, 1888*

"Consecration of Saint Nicholas as Bishop of Myra." Painting by Jean Fouquet.

"The Funeral of Saint Nicholas," with a figure of Christ looking benignly upon the saint in his coffin, flanked by other saints and by mourning men and women. The painting, attributed to an artist of the Veneto-Byzantine School of the eleventh century, is at the Pinacoteca in Lovere. *Frick Art Reference Library, New York*

3. THE THREE GENERALS CONDEMNED TO DEATH

This painting, "Saint Nicholas appearing to Emperor Constantine," by Juan Rexach II, shows the saint hovering over the emperor, as in a dream. The scene illustrates the saint's intervention on behalf of the three generals who had been falsely accused of plotting against Constantine and were facing execution. *Collection of Comte H. de Demandolx-Dedons, Marseilles*

Do you remember seeing three golden balls hanging above the door of a pawnbroker's shop? Did you ever wonder how they became the sign of this particular trade? Well, pawnbrokers and bankers in northern Italy used to look to Saint Nicholas as their patron saint. The sign above their shops symbolized the three bags of gold Nicholas used, while a young man in Myra, to assure the freedom of the three young girls in his hometown. The symbolism of redeeming something of value becomes obvious, once you think about it; in other fields, too, Saint Nicholas was associated with good deeds and miracles in units of three.

The oldest and most detailed of these miracle stories is that of the three *Stratilati* (a word from which "strategy" derives, and which stands for "commanders" or "generals"). This legend is set during the reign of Emperor Constantine when Nicholas was Bishop of Myra, an old and venerable man. The three generals in the story were named Ursos, Nepotianos, and Herpylion. According to a German authority, Karl Meisen, this is "the oldest text concerning Saint Nicholas that exists in Greek tradition." The original document, the *Praxis de Stratilatis,* has been traced to the period of Emperor Justinian (527–565), or shortly thereafter. Meisen believes that "it probably developed in Myra itself for the glorification of its municipal saint."

Not only does the story deal with three generals, it also falls into three parts. In all of them, Saint Nicholas is pictured as the righter of wrongs, either by personal intervention or by such miraculous means as appearance in a dream, or as an apparition. The historical background to the story of the three generals was Emperor Constantine's strenuous effort to retain administrative and military control over outlying provinces of the Roman Empire. In this case, he was faced with a revolt in Phrygia, southeast of Constantinople. This territory contained a mixture of ethnic groups known as the Taiphalis. When news of rebellion against the local administration reached Constantine, he sent the three generals and their troops by ship to the Phrygia region.

Storms forced the expeditionary army to stop over in Andriaki, the port of Myra. With time on their hands, the troops first went into port and then into Myra itself, originally just to buy bread and other provisions. Arguments with tradesmen in Myra's marketplace soon led to fighting between soldiers and the local populace. Looting, destruction, and general rampaging threatened to lead to even more severe violence.

Aware of this danger, Saint Nicholas hurried to the three generals who had remained in port. He asked them, "Who are your Excellencies, and what is your mission?" The generals, respecting the cleric's station, answered, "We are servants of the Emperor as well as of Your Saintliness. By order of the Emperor we are on our way to subdue the Taiphalis. They are in revolt, but bad weather has forced us to stop over here until we can continue our voyage."

To this Bishop Nicholas replied: "You say that the Emperor has instructed you to quiet unrest. How is it, then, that you create troubles in our peaceful town?"

The generals, unaware of their own troops' undisciplined actions, asked, "Who is it that is causing trouble, our Lord Saint?"

Nicholas said: "It is you, because you have permitted your soldiers to loot the public market. The fault is yours."

Hearing this, the generals rushed to Myra's market. Upset by their troops' lack of discipline, they beat some of the soldiers and shouted at others to restore order. While the soldiers joined the townsfolk in repairing the damage, Nicholas invited the three generals to join him at the Cathedral of Myra to eat and drink. The *Vita di Stratilati* adds: "Like a good father, having advised and blessed them, he sent them on their journey. They were happy and pleased, and the Saint walked with them until Andriaki, the port of Myra."

Thus ends the first section of the three-part story. But soon a second crisis arose, and Saint Nicholas was once more called upon to prevent injustice. The *Vita* reports: "The generals were about to return to their ships with their soldiers, ready to depart, and the Saint had started to go back to Myra, when he saw a group of weeping men and women." At that time, the provincial prefect was one Eustathios, a corrupt official, willing to sentence and execute innocent men if bribed by their enemies. That, according to the men and women whom Saint Nicholas encountered, was about to happen. Eustathios had condemned three innocent men to death, and the beheading was about to take place in the center of town. The townspeople had confirmed the complaint of the victim's relatives and guided him to the place of execution.

Taking the three generals with him, Nicholas rushed up to the executioner, tore the sword from his hand, and thus barely prevented a great injustice. Angry and exhausted, he untied the ropes that bound the victims and set them free. News of the event spread like wildfire through Myra and Andriaki. People streamed into the place of execution from all directions.

Alarmed, Prefect Eustathios mounted his horse and joined the crowd. When Saint Nicholas saw him riding onto the square, he stopped the prefect and upbraided him for his corrupt actions. Eustathios admitted he had yielded to threats and bribery by two municipal leaders, Simonedes and Eudoxios. With the three generals present, Nicholas told the prefect that he would inform the emperor of his disgraceful behavior so that Constantine would know personally of his prefect's unworthiness. At that, the account states, Eustathios "was seized by fear, fell on his knees to ask the Saint's pardon and confessed his injustice. Saint Nicholas granted him forgiveness, and they parted in mutual charity."

We now come to the third part of the story. Ursos, Nepotianos, and Herpylion, the three generals, took their troops to Phrygia, successfully crushed the local rebellion, and returned to Constantinople. They reported to Emperor Constantine that their campaign had been "completed without bloodshed." Highly pleased, Emperor Constantine rewarded them with gifts and promoted them to a higher rank.

But their triumph caused envy among rivals at the imperial court, who told Evlavios, the imperial chancellor, that the three generals had given the emperor a totally false account of their Phrygian intervention. Instead of subduing the revolt and strengthening the emperor, the accusers said, the generals had used their soldiers to join the rebellion for personal advantages.

"Are you aware of what these men have actually done?" the chancellor was asked. "The Emperor sent them to subdue the Taiphalis. Instead, they made common cause with these rebels. They even talked their own soldiers into disloyalty to the Emperor, persuaded them to join the Taiphalis, so that they might reign over the territory as Emperors themselves!"

As the Roman Empire was always endangered by just such fragmentation, and as Constantine had consolidated his own power only after he had defeated rival after rival in the eastern and western provinces, such accusations were persuasive. But to make doubly sure the generals would be eliminated, their rivals also bribed Chancellor Evlavios. Even before passing this vicious gossip on to the emperor, Evlavios had the three generals imprisoned although he gave no reason for this surprise action.

Despite the bribe, Evlavios was cautious enough to await direct news from Phrygia before either advising the emperor or taking drastic action against the three generals. Their rivals now became uneasy. They were afraid that their false accusations might be exposed, and so they gave Evlavios still more gold, urging that the generals be put to death quickly; otherwise, they said, the generals might get in touch with the Taiphalis, who then might raid the jail and set them free.

But Evlavios did not want the deaths of the three generals on his hands, nor did he want to repay the bribe money. Instead, he called on the emperor, apparently quite upset, and gave this version of his dilemma:

"Long live the Emperor! The three generals you sent to subdue the Taiphalis did not, I am told, actually carry out your orders. Instead, Ursos, Nepotianos and Herpylion allied themselves with the rebels and are planning to act against your Majesty. I have put them in prison. Your Majesty must decide whether they should be executed for their betrayal, or whether you want to punish them in some other way. In any event, their fate should be a lesson to other would-be traitors."

Emperor Constantine was a man of quick decisions. He assumed that his chancellor's intelligence report was correct and ordered the accused to be executed. Evlavios put the order into writing and sent it into the prison. There the guards told the generals, "You are going to be beheaded tomorrow. Whatever you want to say to your families, or concerning your possessions, you will have to tell us as quickly as possible."

The generals were shocked. They considered themselves the emperor's most reliable commanders. And now, without official accusation or explanation, they had been condemned to death by the very man whose cause they had so skillfully defended! It made no sense, and they were desperate. "How did we offend either God or Emperor," they wondered, "that we should be treated this way? What sin did we commit, that we should have to pay with our lives?"

General Nepotianos said to the other two generals: "At this point, my brothers, human power cannot save us. Remember what happened in Myra of Lycia, where the Great Nicholas saved three men from an unjust death? Perhaps the same can be done to help us out of our desperate dilemma. Surely, no one else can help us. We are bewildered with grief and agony of the heart. Our voices have dried up. Our tongues cannot move. We are not even capable of praying. Come then, let us plead with God and Saint Nicholas. Perhaps the saint will somehow manage to come and save us."

Generals Ursos and Herpylion joined him, with tears in their eyes, and they spoke out loud: "Lord, God of our Father Nicholas who saved the three men of Myra from an unjust death, come in time, Lord, and do not ignore our injustice, nor forget us who are in danger of our lives. Free us from the hands of our enemies. Do not delay, for we are condemned to die tomorrow."

The three imprisoned generals prayed through the night. Shortly before dawn, Emperor Constantine dreamed that a stately figure arose before him and said: "Arise, Emperor. Rise quickly. You must free three men whom you have condemned to death. If you do not do as I say, God will involve you in a war that will result in your own death."

The emperor, not sure whether he was dreaming or seeing the apparition in real life, said, "Who are you to threaten me, and how did you manage to get into the Palace at this hour?"

Nicholas said, "I am the Bishop of Myra, Nicholas, and God has sent me to tell you that these three men must be freed without delay."

The saint also appeared to the imperial chancellor and said, "Evlavios, you who seem to have lost his mind, will you tell me why you permitted yourself to be bribed, and why you have done such grave injury to three innocent men? Free them at once, or I shall ask God to take your life."

Evlavios asked Saint Nicholas who he was, and the saint identified himself in the dream. Evlavios woke up, confused and troubled. But even while he was still lying in bed, trying to shake off the fearful impact of the dream, the chancellor was summoned from his quarters by a palace attendant, who shouted, "Hurry up, the emperor wants you!"

The chancellor rushed over to the emperor, and Constantine told him of his vision. Evlavios confessed that he had virtually the same dream, was puzzled by it, and felt that the three generals should be asked to explain the whole awesome and frightening experience.

When the commanders were brought to the palace, the emperor asked them, "What magic have you been practicing to cause us dreams and sleepless nights?" The generals looked at each other in puzzlement. Filled with fear, they were unable to answer or even to ask the emperor to explain his bewildering question.

Seeing their confusion, Constantine abandoned his brusqueness and said in a more kindly manner, "Go ahead; you may answer without being afraid. I am your friend as well as your emperor."

But the shaken generals still did not know what to make of it all. Having themselves spent a sleepless night, praying, they now thought that they were facing a new accusation: having tried to work a magic spell on the emperor! And they said: "Our Emperor! We have practiced no magic against you. We have never so much as uttered a word against you. In the name of God, we were brought up by our parents to respect God first and our Emperor second. Loyal as we are, we went to Phrygia to deal with the Taiphalis. We scorned all temptations. With God's help, we carried out your instructions, hoping to gain your appreciation. But now we not only face dishonor, but death as well."

The emperor, touched by their obvious sincerity, tried to get to the bottom of the mysterious dream apparition. He asked the men, "Tell me, then, to whom did you appeal for help?" The generals told him of their appeals to God and Saint Nicholas, recalled how they had seen the Bishop of Myra free three men who had been unjustly accused, and said that they hoped he would free them, too, and "clear us of slander and false accusations." The emperor questioned them closely on Nicholas's identity and role in their adventure. General Nepotianos described the events in Myra. They had been particularly impressed, he recalled, that no one, including the Prefect Eustathios, had dared to contradict the bishop. He concluded,

"And so, Oh Emperor of ours, having seen all this with our very own eyes, and remembering how the Saint had rescued these three men, we appealed to God that, through the Saint's prayers, he might help us."

Emperor Constantine assured them that their lives would be spared, "because that Bishop has delivered you from death." He told them to become monks because of this miraculous rescue, to visit Saint Nicholas and tell him that he, Constantine, had obeyed him and that "he should not threaten me anymore."

Constantine gave them a gold-covered Bible, a golden incense vessel covered with precious stones, and two gold-plated candlesticks. All these were to be taken to the cathedral at Myra.

The three generals gave their personal possessions to the poor and to their relatives, and they became monks. They collected other gifts for the church where Nicholas was bishop, and they set sail for Myra. Bishop Nicholas received them gracefully but brushed away all their thanks to him personally. Instead, he urged them to praise the Lord who had miraculously saved them from an unjust fate. Thus ends the oldest of the triple miracles attributed to Saint Nicholas.

Saint Nicholas is shown here as physically grasping the sword with which the executioner is about to behead one of the three falsely condemned men. The painting, by Lorenzo di Niccolò, is at the Pinacoteca Vaticana. *Anderson-Alinari*

Notable for its striking perspective, this work of Paolo Veronese is entitled "Saint Nicholas Receiving Dignitaries at Myra." It is in the possession of the Royal Academy of Fine Arts, Venice. *Alinari*

Four scenes from the life of Saint Nicholas. Upper left: the infant standing upright in his bath; lower left: Nicholas is made Bishop of Myra; upper right: he rescues sailors at sea; lower right: the saint protects three falsely accused men from execution. The scenes are contained in a twelfth-century manuscript found in the Benedictine Abbey at Lambach, Austria, from where they were transferred to the State Library in Berlin, Germany.

Traditional Greek image of Saint Nicholas, as shown in an anonymous icon at the Eastern Orthodox Monastery on Mount Athos, Greece. *Nicholas Tombazi, Psychico-Athens*

4. THE FIGHTING SAINT

This drawing depicts the saint in spiritual combat with the Devil, or a diabolical figure, seeking to bend the mast of a ship and destroy its crew (upper right). Saint Nicholas (center left) is shown as he blesses the endangered sailors who look up and appeal to him. The work, by Albrecht Altdorfer, is entitled "Miracle of Saint Nicholas: Shipwrecked Sailors." *Ashmolean Museum, Oxford*

Saint Nicholas emerges from several legends as impatient, forceful, and occasionally angry; he was a fighting saint. This is vividly illustrated by his participation in the First Council of Nicaea. The council codified Christian thought for many centuries; from it emerged the Nicene Creed, which remains a key document to the present day.

The council met in the summer of the year 325. Its sessions probably began on June 19 and ended on August 25. The meeting coincided with the twentieth anniversary of the rule of Emperor Constantine over the Roman Empire. The emperor's influence was strongly felt throughout the meeting. Constantine's triumphs had made him protector of all Christians in the empire. Earlier, wave after wave of persecutions had weakened Christianity, but during Constantine's rule Christianity had become the dominant religion of the empire.

Constantine, the first Christian emperor, was a man of strong political instincts, anxious to be—as ruler over fifty million diverse subjects—all things to all men. He had adopted Christianity, but did not wish to alienate pagans and other non-Christians within the far-flung empire. His own baptism did not take place until shortly before his death. His leading role within the Christian communities often reflected political needs rather than theological judgment.

Saint Nicholas's own lifetime closely paralleled Constantine's rule. He was perhaps in his mid-forties when he was called to attend the First Council of Nicaea. Bishops from all parts of the Roman Empire, mainly from the eastern rather than the western regions, assembled in this Asia Minor town. All told, more than three hundred church leaders—the exact figure may have been 318—made the long sea and land voyages to attend the meeting. For Saint Nicholas the trip from Myra to Nicaea may have lasted about two weeks.

What caused Emperor Constantine to summon the bishops of the Christian church to Nicaea?

One technical but basic question was the date on which Easter should be celebrated by Christians throughout the empire. Some areas preferred to hold celebrations on the same date on which Passover was being celebrated by the Jewish communities; others thought it more appropriate that Easter be fixed on a specific day of the week. The Sunday following Passover was preferred. On this, agreement was reached at Nicaea.

But a more profound theological question was in dispute, one which had really begun to threaten the unity of the Christian community: the divinity of Christ. Emperor Constantine favored Christianity within his empire because it was a widespread but unified faith. He was distressed by a split that threatened Christian unity.

As far as Saint Nicholas was concerned, there was no doubt where his adherence belonged. He sided with what emerged as the majority of the bishops at Nicaea. The opposing view concerning Christ's divinity was expressed by a leading priest in Alexandria, Arian. According to one historian, Isaac Boyle, the emperor had hardly managed to subdue his external enemies when the theological debate threatened internal conflict: "The Church was protected from its foreign enemies, a dissension had arisen in its own bosom, which occasioned much animosity and long continued to disturb its domestic peace." Constantine had subdued his last rival, Licinius, only two years earlier, in 323. The council now gave him an opportunity to bring church leaders together while strengthening his own control within the church. Nicholas of Myra, whose fame did not unfold until after his death, in centuries to come, attended the council as an equal among equals.

The dispute concerning the divinity of Christ was so intricate, so closely linked with the use and meaning of specific Greek words, that it is difficult to summarize. Basically, Arian maintained that Jesus had been created by God; that Jesus had not existed before, although God had existed forever. This suggested, in turn, that Jesus was not as God, was not his equal, was not co-equal, and that therefore "the Son has a beginning, but God is without beginning." Arian used these words in a letter to his ally, Bishop Eusebius of Nicomedia. Arian's chief opponent was his own superior, Alexander, Bishop of Alexandria, who referred to Arian and his supporters as "iniquitous men, and enemies of Christ, teaching an Apostasy which might be justly thought and called a forerunner of the Antichrist."

This was the setting Nicholas faced at Nicaea:

Preliminary exchanges of views had been completed. The

formal session had begun. The great hall of the palace at Nicaea was filled with visiting bishops and the emperor's attendants. Benches were stretched out to either side of the emperor, whose chair was elevated in the center of the room and covered with gold leaf. Constantine was dressed in a robe of purple and gold. The formal presentation of the opposing views began with a speech by Bishop Alexander, followed by a talk given by Arian himself.

The Athenian monk Damaskinos, in 1896, published this version of the event:

"The Emperor was now sitting on his throne, flanked by 159 Bishops to his left and 159 to his right. Arian was presenting his views with great vigor and detail. As Saint Nicholas observed the scene, the Bishops listened to Arian in complete silence and without interrupting this discourse. Outraged, and prompted by his saintly vigor, he left his seat and walked up to Arian, faced him squarely and slapped his face.

"At this, the assembly was shocked. Arian's supporters turned to the Emperor, asking that he intervene and punish Nicholas. They said, 'Oh Just One, tell us, can it be fair that in your very presence someone should be permitted, without hindrance, to assault another? If he has anything to say in rebuttal, by all means let him have his say. But if he is not sufficiently learned to make a proper argument, then it were better if he remain in his seat, quietly, and listen to others who are prepared to state their case in words.'

"Arian himself spoke directly to the Emperor, 'Should anyone who has the temerity to hit me, in front of Your Majesty, remain unpunished?' Emperor Constantine replied, 'Indeed, there is a law which forbids anyone to lift his hand in violence in the presence of the Emperor and it specifies that his hand be cut off. However, it is not up to me, in this Assembly, to act upon it. Instead, you, Your Holinesses, should make the decision in this case; I leave it to your judgment, whether and how this act is to be punished.'

"The Bishops conferred with each other, and when they came to a decision, they said to the Emperor, 'Your Majesty, the Bishop of Myra has acted wrongfully. We all saw it happen and attest to it. We therefore ask your permission to let us strip him of his clerical garments, shackle him and place him under guard as a prisoner. In this way, he shall not be permitted to partici-

pate in the proceedings of the Council for the rest of our delib-
erations. Once the synod is completed, a final judgment in this
case may be made.'

"As a result, that evening, Nicholas was made a prisoner in
another wing of the Palace. He was placed in a jail-like room,
without his bishop's mantle and shackled on hand and foot.
However, during the night he was visited by Jesus Christ and
the Holy Mother. They observed Saint Nicholas in his cell and
said, 'Nicholas, why are you imprisoned?' And Saint Nicholas
said, 'Because of my love for you.' First they freed him from his
shackles. And then Jesus said, 'Take this!' and he gave him a
volume of the Holy Scripture. Then the Holy Mother went
away, returned, and brought him his bishop's garments, so that
he might clothe himself with appropriate dignity. At peace, he
studied the Holy Book through the night.

"The next morning, a jailer came to bring him bread, saw that
Nicholas was no longer shackled, that he was clothed in the
garments of his position, and that he was studying the Scriptures in his cell. Even his stole was in his one hand, while he
held the book with the other. News of this miraculous event was
quickly brought to the Emperor. He asked that Nicholas be
freed, and when the two men met, the Emperor asked the
Bishop's forgiveness."

The meeting's decision was on the side which Nicholas of
Myra favored. Attendance records of the First Council of
Nicaea are the main proof for the historical existence of Nicholas, Bishop of Myra. The event ended with a grand banquet,
given by the emperor, who presented every one of the bishops
with a valuable gift before their voyage home.

Nicholas probably arrived back in Myra early in September,
having been away from his flock for some two months. Saint
Nicholas's role as a fighting saint, dramatized at Nicaea, was felt
in Myra as well. During his lifetime and in centuries after his
death, Christianity was in conflict with the pagan traditions of
Greece and Rome. Throughout the province of Lycia, habits of
pagan venerations had been ingrained for millennia. Legend
has it that Saint Nicholas was, in life and beyond death, at war
with the ancient Greek goddess Artemis. As religious faith suc-
ceeds religious faith, one man's god becomes another man's
demon; and so Nicholas saw the influence of the Artemis image
as demon-inspired. The saint's healing powers are frequently

described as due to his ability to oust demons from the bodies of possessed men and women.

Artemis-worship continued in Myra during Nicholas's period as the town's Christian bishop. He had to keep parishioners from sliding back into pagan habits of ritual and allegiance. No doubt, some of them, although nominally Christian, secretly visited Myra's Temple of Artemis for sacrifice and prayer to benefit from the goddess's healing power.

Greek mythology speaks of Artemis, a daughter of Zeus, as gifted with manifold powers. Rivalry, at least in a symbolic sense, is certainly indicated when one recalls the saint's special role as patron of sailors. Artemis was, among other things, the goddess of seafarers, bestower of fair weather and successful sea voyages. She is also mentioned as a harvest goddess and protector of grain. In addition to several stories that speak of Saint Nicholas as the guardian of sailors, there is also a legend that credits him with powers to multiply grain during a period of famine.

The legends concerning Nicholas and Artemis speak of fierce warfare between the two, which even outlasted Nicholas's lifetime. The *Vita Compilata* says that Nicholas was so infuriated by the presence of the Temple of Artemis in Myra that he destroyed it with his own hands. As the temple was inhabited by a demon whose allegiance was to Artemis, who sought to prevent the bishop from carrying out his plan, the account suggests virtual physical combat between Nicholas and the resident demon.

Saint Nicholas was frustrated by the continued presence and influence of the Artemis structure. If it followed the pattern of numerous temples dedicated to this goddess all over the Middle East, it consisted of large grounds, complete with plants designed to keep the earth fresh, an inner court surrounded by columns, an altar, and a statue of Artemis (who, often regarded as equivalent to the Roman goddess Diana, protectress of wild creatures and the hunt, was later pictured with bow and arrow). This account noted that the saint wanted, literally, to uproot the Artemis cult and that he "destroyed it, angrily, down to its very foundations, which he tore out of the ground." The resident demon was ousted and condemned to roam the earth.

But the struggle lasted beyond Saint Nicholas's life and included a planned attack on his tomb in Myra. The tomb, large and appropriately decorated, possibly with a chapel attached, was a popular visiting point for pilgrims to Myra. There they prayed for the saint's blessing and patronage, asked for healings, or for protection before going on a potentially dangerous sea journey.

One such boatload of pilgrims had an extraordinary experience several years after the saint's death. They departed from a coastal area, or from an island, planning to visit the saint's tomb, taking with them various gifts to honor the saint and ask his protection. The following account of this voyage appears in the *Vita Per Michaelem:*

"He, our Saintly Father and Christ's universally acclaimed hierarch, and now passed on to the Lord, following the many miraculous acts of his lifetime, continued to demonstrate magnificently his praiseworthy piety even after his death. He thereby caused wonder among the groups of the faithful living in every land and province who joined in honoring and worshiping him. Some came from foreign and distant lands to demonstrate their admiration for the saint, seeking to have their minds enlightened by his saintly grace. Among them was one group, now engaged in preparing to pay homage at his sweet-smelling and illness-healing resting place.

"While these faithful were making preparations for their journey, their activity was noted by an evil and ruthless demon who at one time had inhabited the Temple of Artemis, an edifice that had been cleared of his demonic presence by our saintly and miracle-performing father and his supporters. Now, then, as these pilgrims were about to set out on their journey to the city of Myra, the demon approached them, having taken on the appearance of a woman. In this disguise, the demon spoke to the travelers and claimed that she had hoped to make the journey with them, but, being unable to do so, handed them a container that she said was filled with olive oil.

"She said to the pilgrims: 'Take this container, oh men, as I am in ill health and cannot bring this offering to the saint myself. Please forgive my illness, which prevents me from going with you to your destination. Once you have reached this much-venerated site, please pour this oil into the lamps that burn at the sacred place.'

"This, however, was pretense. The container (shaped like a wine skin, which could be used for any sort of liquid), although it seemed to contain oil, was actually filled with a liquid of evil and maleficent power. The demons who had been driven out of the Temple of Artemis had been unable to harm the saint during his lifetime, despite many attempts; now, these evil creatures, filled with resentment and rancor, were about to prove their criminal nature once again, this time hoping to use the pilgrims to destroy the glorious grave and the saintly relics it contained.

"Having received this supposed offering, the travelers set out on their journey, carrying the container the evil spirit had given them, and setting their sails toward Myra. They spent all of the first day at sea. At night, however, Nicholas himself, the ever-present fervent defender of the victims of evil, appeared to one of the victims of the diabolical plan, and said to him: 'Rise up and hurl this alien container to the bottom of the sea!' At dawn, the man carried out this command he had received in his sleep, and he threw the vessel into the water.

"The moment he had done this, a huge flame rose into the air and remained suspended above the ocean, emitting dense smoke and nauseating odors. At the same time, the sea was torn asunder and began to boil with a great roaring noise, while drops of water were flung about like flaming sparks. The travelers were awed and frightened by this terrible sight. The whole boat on which they were assembled now shuddered in the turbulent water. The crew members, frightened by the sight and overcome by the foul smells, abandoned the boat's helm and oars. Both crew and passengers were overcome by fear for their safety.

"Soon, however, their Protector [Saint Nicholas] was able to quiet their fears, as he commanded the satanic upheaval to yield by sinking to the bottom of the sea. Realizing that they had thus been saved, the men became aware that this danger and threat to their lives had been the demon's work. Not long after, they were able to reach the shore, disembark, and now the men were at last fully free of fear. Seized by great joy, they gave their thanks to God and Saint Nicholas—to the first as Creator and Guardian of his creature, and to the second as the mediator who had caused their remarkable salvation by God."

There is a consistency in these two separate accounts, which suggests that there was active Artemis worship in Lycia and that transition from the worship of Greek and Roman gods and goddesses was turbulent. While we cannot be sure of Nicholas's actual life span, it seems likely that he lived during the tumultuous period that brought Christianity to sudden prominence. The *Vita Per Metaphrasten* suggests that the anti-Christian decrees issued by Emperor Constantine's predecessors directly affected Nicholas. These predecessors were Diocletian (245–313), emperor from 284 to 305, and Maximilianus, who ruled the empire's western territories from 286 to 305.

Diocletian claimed to be a descendant of Jupiter and demanded that he be worshiped as a god. The empire's Christians had not opposed his secular authority but balked at this request. Diocletian went into a fury of frustration. In 303 he ordered Christian churches and sacred books burned. He demanded that Christians either give up their faith or be enslaved, imprisoned, and tortured.

If Nicholas was Bishop of Myra during the closing years of the reign of Diocletian, his community was doubtlessly affected by these decrees. The persecutions lasted, beyond Diocletian's resignation (305), until 311, when Nicholas may have been thirty-one years old. If he had suffered the violence inflicted by predecessors of Constantine, his anger directed against the Temple of Artemis becomes understandable.

Simeon Metaphrastes writes that Diocletian appointed district governors "who spread the news that whoever was a Christian, if he renounced Christ he would have great honors from the Emperor but if he insisted on his Christian faith and showed no respect for the pagan idols, would be punished and tortured." He adds, describing the conditions under which Nicholas functioned: "Many of the Christians then admitted boldly that Christ was the true God, and died after suffering great torture; but, alas, others renounced Christ out of fear and made sacrifices to idols. There were also those who were afraid, but who neither wished to renounce Christ nor make sacrifices to the idols, and these people hid themselves in caves on the mountains." Simeon writes:

"The orders of the Emperor also reached Myra, the very Bishopric of the Saint, and when the governors found the Saint they made him suffer torment and cast him into prison with the other Christians. While in prison, the Saint gladly suffered all inflictions, such as thirst and hunger. He remained in jail for considerable time, where he urged others to be firm in their faith."

When Constantine became emperor and reversed these rulings, "all Christians were freed from their prisons, including, of course, Saint Nicholas, who was reinstated as Bishop and Shepherd of the Myraians." The Temple of Artemis is described as "a great pagan altar, bigger than all others in height and width."

Saint Nicholas, according to this version, did not destroy the temple physically. Simeon Metaphrastes writes: "As soon as the Saint began praying, the altar collapsed, and the statues of idols fell down, like leaves of a tree when a strong wind blows in autumn. The demons who inhabited the place left, but protested to the Saint amidst their tears: 'You have been unjust to us. We did you no harm, and yet you send us away from our home. We had made this our home, while these misguided people adored us, and now where can we go?' And the Saint replied, 'Go to Hell's fire, which has been lit for you by the devil and his crew.' In this manner, all altars in the area were destroyed."

Saint Nicholas's patronage of sailors has suggested to some historians that elements of Poseidon, Greek god of the sea, were transferred to Nicholas. The same, as we have seen, applied to characteristics of Artemis, including that of guardian of grain. In view of this, the story of the multiplied grain is significant. This is one of the oldest Saint Nicholas legends. Three early Byzantine versions exist.

The first legend speaks of a famine in Lycia, during which Bishop Nicholas frantically tried to obtain grain for the province. When several ships, on their way from Alexandria to Constantinople and loaded with grain, arrived at Andriaki, Nicholas hurried to the port. He urged the captain of the ships to set aside a part of their load for Lycia. But the captains refused, saying that the loads had been weighed carefully and they would be held responsible for any shortages on delivery. However, the bishop assured them there would be no such repercussions, and they finally agreed to set aside one hundred bushels of grain from each ship. Miraculously, when the ships arrived at Constantinople, the grain weighed exactly what it had before. And when Saint Nicholas distributed the grain in Lycia, it lasted for two years, and there was enough left to serve as seed for future harvests.

Another version speaks of a famine during which Nicholas appeared to the captain of a passing grain ship as a merchant. He bought grain from the captain, handing him three gold coins and telling him to take the boat to Myra. When the captain awoke, the next morning, he thought he had dreamed the whole episode. However, he actually held three gold coins in his hand and changed the ship's course to take the grain to Myra. In an elaboration of this version, the ship was on its way to France when Saint Nicholas prompted it to change course; the three gold coins were a down payment, a gesture of good will to assure the captain that he would later be paid in full.

The third version, like the story of the demon's plot against Saint Nicholas's grave, is placed after the saint's death. It states that five years after he died, there was a dangerous famine. Nicholas appeared as an apparition to a family member, Theodolus, and urged him to hold a service of petition at the saint's tomb in Myra. The congregation complied, there was a fierce earthquake at midnight, the coffin opened, and an odor of myrrh came from it that satiated the starving and helped the blind and the lame.

A few days later, Nicholas appeared as a patriarch, carrying a mitre that seemed to be made of fiery flames. He walked across the water to board five grain ships traveling from Cyprus to Constantinople. He purchased grain, made a down payment, and urged the captains to take their boats to Myra. But the Devil convinced them that the whole thing was a fraud, and they refused to change course. When a storm arose, which then quieted down, they changed their minds and followed Saint Nicholas's orders. They landed in Myra, calmed the fleeing population, told them what had happened, and sold the grain. When they visited the coffin of Nicholas, they recognized that it was he who had appeared to them; they placed the down payment on his grave as an offering, and the people held a feast in his honor.

The grain story has inspired many paintings. Two Italian masters have dealt with this theme in detail. Ambrogio Lorenzetti's work, in the *Reale Galleria antica e moderna* in Florence, shows how a boatload of grain is transferred from one ship, lying in a port, to a smaller vessel. Two angels can be seen overhead: they pour grain into the big ship to replace the load it is discharging. Ashore is Saint Nicholas who, surrounded by the dignitaries, observes the miraculous replacement of grain.

Another painting, by Fra Angelico, is in the Pinacoteca of the Vatican, and it obviously illustrates the third, or post mortem, version of the legend. The picture is in three parts. On the left is a port, with one ship anchored, while a second is just about to come in. In the background is a town with walls, towers, gates, and a fortress. On the shore, Bishop Nicholas, accompanied by another cleric, speaks to the ship owner. To the right of this scene are two dock workers who shovel grain into sacks, while others carry filled sacks into the town. A third section shows a third ship, with five people visible on board, which is moving backward with its sails filled with wind. Nicholas can be seen above, surrounded by a halo of rays, apparently driving the ship into the proper direction; up front, a monster sticks its head out of the water, probably symbolizing the Devil who sought to convince the captain not to send his boat to Myra.

Saint Nicholas emerges from these legends as a forceful and resourceful protagonist, a fighting saint who defeated his enemies, and who stood by his people in times of need—by normal as well as miraculous means, during his lifetime, and even after his death.

One exorcism legend that developed in the Ukraine and Russia, but was neither recorded nor depicted in Western Europe, concerns the banishment of the Devil from a well. This fifteenth-century Russian icon shows the Devil, small and black, emerging from waves atop the well. *The Russian Museum, Leningrad*

Several legends speak of Saint Nicholas's antagonism to Artemis, the Hellenic goddess, her temple in Myra, where Nicholas was bishop, and the demons said to be attached to the goddess. This statue of Artemis illustrates the role of the goddess as earth mother, nourishing nature with her multiple breasts. The statue was excavated and is on display at Ephesus. *Turkish Information Office*

The famous and beautiful *Book of Hours* of Jean, Duke of Berry, contains this drawing of Saint Nicholas as he stops a storm at sea, one of the earliest legends concerning the saint. The fifteenth-century book was prepared by Pol, Jean, and Herman de Limbourg, and is dated for the period from 1410 to 1413. *The Metropolitan Museum of Art, New York. The Cloisters Collection, Purchase, 1954*

The role of Saint Nicholas as the patron of sailors has been depicted in many paintings. It is the link between the Byzantine and the early West European, notably Italian, concepts of the saint. The sea-oriented Mediterranean tradition is well expressed in Lorenzo di Bicci's "Saint Nicholas Saving the Mariners." *Ashmolean Museum, Oxford*

Sailors in distress, about to be rescued by Saint Nicholas. Scene from a fresco depicting several legends of the saint. The artist belonged to the Veronese School of the fourteenth century. From the collection of San Zeno Maggiore, Verona. *Frick Art Reference Library, New York*

The miracle of the grain shipment is depicted in this painting by Fra Angelico. Saint Nicholas is shown twice, participating (left, foreground) in the transfer of the grain, while (upper right) he is suspended in the air and his whole body surrounded by a halo, as he directs the ship and protects the billowing sails and mast against demons and elements. Pinacoteca Vaticana, Vatican City. *Alinari*

Saint Nicholas, responding to the prayers of the people suffering from famine, is the theme of this painting by Flemish artist Otto Venius (Van Veen). *Royal Museum of Fine Arts, Antwerp*

5. SAINT NICHOLAS TO THE RESCUE!

The son who had been kidnaped from Myra, on the saint's feast day, was returned miraculously to his parents one year later. This painting, from the Study of Luca Signorelli (1441–1523), shows the boy (foreground) as he hands a cup of wine to his master. Saint Nicholas is about to lift him up and transport him back to his father and mother. In the background (right) the parents are shown kneeling as the saint returns their son to them. *The High Museum of Art, Atlanta. Gift of the Samuel Kress Foundation, 1958*

Some years after the death of Saint Nicholas, the townspeople of Myra were celebrating his memory on the eve of his nameday, December 6, with eating, drinking, and a generally festive air. Unarmed and unaware of events around them, the townspeople did not realize that a band of Arab pirates from Crete had landed on their shore and was making its way into Myra. The pirates even managed to get into the Church of Saint Nicholas itself to collect booty in the form of chalices, altar decoration, and bejeweled icons. As they left town, they took along the son of a local peasant, Basilios, as a slave.

When the pirates returned to their home island, the emir of Crete selected young Basilios to be his personal cupbearer. He became part of the emir's elaborate court and household, while in Myra his disconsolate parents mourned their son as if he had died. His mother was so deeply grieved that she could no longer think of festivities in honor of Saint Nicholas as anything but a day of tragedy. The following year, she at first refused to take place in the nameday celebrations at all. Finally her husband convinced her to participate in the feast, although she could not bring herself to join the festive crowd in the town square. The feastday was celebrated quietly at home.

Just as family and guests sat down to the evening meal, the dogs began to bark fiercely in the courtyard; something startling had been seen or scented by them. The head of the family moved cautiously to the courtyard door—and there, to his amazement bordering on terror, he saw his son, dressed in an Arab tunic and holding a full wine goblet in his hand.

What contributed to the startling nature of this ghostlike appearance was Basilios's rigid stance. He stared uncomprehendingly into space, immovable and unspeaking. At last, when the son realized that he was in his father's house, back home in Myra, father and son joined the rest of the family. The ghostly visitor was as real as he had ever been, and eventually he told the story of his miraculous reappearance.

Basilios recalled that he had been busy at his job with the emir of Crete, selecting wines, pouring them, carrying cups to the emir and his entourage. While engrossed in this routine, he suddenly felt himself uplifted, removed from the emir's palace, carried away by an invisible power, and naturally frightened. Just as he was about to despair, and in fear of his life, Saint Nicholas appeared. Facing the boy, the saint blessed and encouraged young Basilios and led him back to the home of his family in Myra.

The feastday was now more than ever a day of praise and rejoicing in Basilios's family; the whole town joined in prayers of thanks to God and to the saint who had been bishop of their town during his lifetime.

The purity and simplicity of this story makes it one of the most appealing of the Saint Nicholas legends. As the saint's worship and patronates made their way to the European West, the legend underwent a number of variations in the retelling and rewriting, but its essence remained unchanged. For example, one of the best-known compilers and elaborators, John Diaconus, speaks of a pilgrim to Myra, who arrived at his destination just as Saint Nicholas was to be buried. The pilgrim, Cethron, husband of Euprosina of Exoranda, had hoped to obtain Nicholas's blessings toward the conception and birth of a son.

Cethron was able to obtain a relic of the saint. He took it back to Exoranda, hoping that his prayers might be answered by the saint's miraculous powers, even after his bodily death. On the urging of his wife, he built a chapel dedicated to Saint Nicholas, just outside of town. The church was dedicated by the local bishop, Apollonius. The relic, noted for its delicate scent, showed miraculous qualities.

Symbolizing the saint's intervention on the devoted family's behalf, a son was born on Saint Nicholas's feastday. The boy was named Adeodatus. From then on, the family celebrated their son's birth on the saint's nameday. When Adeodatus was seven years old, and while everyone was preparing for Saint Nicholas Day, the town was invaded by Arabs. Many inhabitants were kidnaped, to be taken into slavery, and transported to Babylon; among them was the young boy. When the prisoners were divided among the leading Arab families, Adeodatus was taken on as cupbearer in the palace of King Marmorinus.

One year later, when Saint Nicholas Day came around once more, a startling event took place. Adeodatus had served the king well, and the royal ruler had just told the boy that no force in the world would separate them. At that moment, as the young cupbearer had filled a goblet with wine and was just handing it to King Marmorinus, boy and cup disappeared into thin air. They rematerialized in the youngster's hometown, in the midst of his family. The rest of the story corresponds to the earlier Eastern version.

The story of the kidnaped boy became a popular miracle play in the twelfth and thirteenth centuries. Aside from its exotic locale, pious orientation, and moral uplift, the play had striking personalities and an attention-holding plot. It was adapted to various settings and regions. In one version, the boy was depicted as of Norman origin.

Two Vatican manuscripts offer still another variation. In this case, a widow by the name of Constantiai is the mother of three boys. While they are preparing for Nicholas's feast day, the youngest of the three is kidnaped. He is imprisoned and out of reach of normal rescue procedure. Saint Nicholas, however, by adopting the identity of a young man, is able to free the child and return him to his mother and brothers.

The legend of the kidnaped son has not been pictured with great frequency. One painting, by Giottini, is to be found in the Lower Church of Saint Francis in Assisi. The kidnaped boy is shown in a subdued pose, his arms crossed before his chest, standing before a king and queen who face him across a table covered with food and drink. Next, a panel shows the king at a smaller table, while the boy approaches him bearing a cup; Saint Nicholas floats above the boy, his hands behind the youngster's head, ready to lift him up and carry him away.

The three versions of this story illustrate, once again, the multiple link between Saint Nicholas and young children. In the legends concerning the kidnaping, the saint is obviously the protector and rescuer of an innocent child. In the variation that gives him the name Adeodatus, this is combined with Nicholas in the role of interceding for a childless couple praying for a boy child. This fertility theme is the same as in the legend of Nicholas's own birth (and that of Samuel in the Old Testament, to which it has been linked): a barren woman prays for a child, and her prayers are answered, either directly by God or through saintly intercession.

This theme has given rise to psychological interpretations of Saint Nicholas, not as a mere patron of children, but as a fertility symbol. Dr. Adriaan de Groot, professor of psychology, University of Amsterdam, has noted that, "In the Middle Ages, St. Nicholas was not only the protector of children but also the patron of parenthood, the fosterer of family fertility. He must have been invoked many, many times by married couples who wanted children." Beyond this, particularly in France, churches dedicated to Saint Nicholas were visited by young women who asked the saint's intercession to find a husband.

We must not look for a direct line between Eastern and Western, between Mediterranean and European attitudes toward the saint. His personality, his patronates, and the legends surrounding him added to the image of the saint without clearcut chronology and logical progression. Yet, the stories of the kidnaped boy have a universal theme and appeal: a child is forcibly removed from his parents, a period of despair and mourning passes, and the boy is miraculously returned. Here we find Saint Nicholas quite clearly as the Guardian of Children, a patronate more profound and humanly valuable, one might say, than a mere Giver of Gifts.

The patronate of Saint Nicholas over children had many aspects. At one time or another, it ranged from courtship and a desire for marriage up to the protection of children against all dangers, including death. The saint could be a mediator of a young woman's prayer for a suitor and subsequent marriage, the conception of a child and its safe birth and babyhood, protection during student years and against all vicissitudes, including illness, kidnaping, and early death.

The fertility theme is illustrated by the case of Nicholas of Tolentino who lived in northern Italy at Sant'Angelo, near Termo (Ancona) in the late twelfth century. Legend had it that he was given the name Nicholas because his parents asked Saint Nicholas, then of Bari, to help them conceive a child. Husband and wife saw an angel in their dreams who told them that they should make a pilgrimage to Bari and visit the tomb of Nicholas. They did so and had a vision of the saint who promised them a son, to be called Nicholas. Eventually, when this son had passed through life, a chapel was built over his grave in his native Tolentino. The wall fresco within the chapel depicts scenes from the life of Saint Nicholas, among them a picture showing the father and mother praying to the saint.

Particularly colorful was the fairly recent practice in France

which seemed to combine pre-Christian traditions with Saint
Nicholas worship. One center of such worship was the dramati-
cally located Chapelle St.-Nicholas-des-Bois-aux-Biards in Normandy, situated on a rock outcropping. Young women went on
pilgrimages to this chapel, appealing to Saint Nicholas for the
fulfillment of their romantic-marital desires. Equally minded
marriageable women had to climb, with a good deal of skill and
daring, to reach the top of a monolith at Notre-Dame de Déliv-
erance, in Cenaye near Bayeux in the Department of Calvados;
once there, they had to put a coin into a monolith, and only then
could they expect to encounter a marriageable male.

These practices are characteristic of long-forgotten, and possibly pagan, rituals with sexually symbolic overtones. Elements
of ambivalence toward Saint Nicholas are shown in other practices. Thus, marriageable maidens at Fécamp Seine-Intérieure
used to throw pebbles at a statue of Saint Nicholas, to gain his
attention in the manner of a child or suitor who throws small
stones at a windowpane. And in the Department of Seine-et-
Marne, young women in the town of Provins used to jiggle the
lock at the local Saint Nicholas chapel, reciting the childlike
verse: *Patron des filles, saint Nicholas: mariez-nous, ne tardez
pas*, which means, "Saint Nicholas, patron of girls: get me married without delay." Married women yearning for a child went
through a similar ritual. In fact, in all of Normandy and in many
other French regions, this jingle used to be quite popular: *Saint
Nicholas, marie les filles avec les garcons*, which translates simply, "Saint Nicholas, marry the girls to the boys."

Similar rituals have been practiced, or remain in practice, in
parts of Holland, Belgium, Germany, and the Scandinavian
countries. Despite the popularity of Saint Nicholas of Bari in
Italy, similar practices have not taken root, or simply have not
been widely reported from Italy. On the other hand, in the
town of Hellerup Danish girls who were about to be married
used to decorate the Saint Nicholas portrait in a local church
with flowers each Saturday.

The patronate of Saint Nicholas over happy marriages
gradually widened into the idea that the saint tended to in-
spire happiness and wealth, so that Saint Nicholas Day eventually became generally regarded as lucky. As a result, the
sixth of December was accepted as the kind of "lucky day"
on which important business transactions, purchases, and
marriages took place.

These romantic and mundane rituals, a merger of various Saint Nicholas patronates, reflect the early legend of the three poverty-stricken girls whom Saint Nicholas helped with three bags of coins, although adapted and expanded into a wider patronate and image of all-around good fortune. Of course, we also find in them the basis for the saint's later development into a Giver of Gifts. After all, the young woman was asking him for the "gift" of a husband; the mother-to-be, for the "gift" of a child; and those imploring the saint for good fortune were hoping for a "gift" in one form or another.

The kidnaped boy who is returned, miraculously, through the intervention of Saint Nicholas also represents a gift, so to speak, from heaven—an unexpected, much-desired good fortune that is bestowed on those of unwavering faith. The ultimate gift, the "gift of life," is illuminated in a rather violent, even macabre, story that shows Saint Nicholas as the rescuer of three young students. It touches on two major themes in the saint's image: the patronage of children and the frequency with which the number three is used. Three young theology students stopped at a country inn for the night. While they were asleep, the innkeeper rifled their belongings. When he discovered that they were carrying a large sum of money, he robbed them and killed them. Then he took the three bodies, cut them up, salted the flesh, and put it in pickle barrels.

Some time later Saint Nicholas stopped at the inn. He sensed or knew what had happened, located the barrels, miraculously reconstituted the three students, and brought them back to life.

While some manuscripts simply speak of the youngsters as students, a number of paintings show their heads shaven in the manner of a monk's tonsure. The legend's impact has mainly been visual. Hundreds of paintings, sculptures, stained-glass windows, and bas-reliefs depicting this story can be found all over Europe. The story was the subject of numerous miracle play productions; that it was regarded as eminently worthy of artistic reproduction is, in itself, an indication of its hold on the public imagination. The scene used to illustrate the legend was usually Saint Nicholas standing over the three boys as they emerged, naked, from their barrels, in many instances with their hands held up in prayer. In nearly all cases, they are shown as very small, although often with quite mature features, the saint hovering over them in larger-than-life size.

Reconstitution of dismembered bodies into living, breathing, unharmed human beings reflects an acceptance of the miraculous that was not easily comprehended in the period of the Early Church. What, then, gave the legend of the three students such cultural strength? What need did it fulfill? Why was it created in the first place?

Meisen explains how this legend could have originated in northern France in the twelfth century. He writes:

"The position of Nicholas as patron saint of students, unknown within the Greek Nicholas cult, which is expressed in this legend, must have arisen in the West about this time. It seems that the concept of student patronage came first, and the legend of the murdered and then revived students came later. This would be the reverse of other cases, where a legend established the foundation for Saint Nicholas as patron saint of a specific profession or other group in the West. We must, therefore, look for different motives as well. And we can note that the specific conditions in northern France in the twelfth century did indeed develop from unique cultural developments."

Northern France was then the center of new spiritual, cultural, and artistic European initiatives, a period of early Renaissance. Young men in search of knowledge and stimulation were traveling to the region in large number. The educational institutions of northern France included a number of cathedral and bishopric schools. Travel was risky, and the young students could well have been in special need of the protection offered by a patron saint of the type other professions enjoyed and worshiped.

Meisen notes that, during the closing years of the eleventh century and the beginning of the twelfth, "The cult of Nicholas made enormous inroads all over France, so that it was quite natural that one should turn toward this saint whose life story provided traditional elements that could be utilized in developing a new patronate." The German historian draws attention to a sermon by Nicholas of Clairvaux, apparently delivered during the second quarter of the twelfth century, which eulogized the saint for his service to the young, both male and female, and for his particular help to those eager to better themselves by education in the divine services.

The sermon was preached during a service at a Clairvaux convent, an educational center of the clergy, and it specifically appealed to young students planning to become priests. Inasmuch as, Meisen writes, "the boys and young men attending the convent schools were for the most part aiming at an ecclesiastical career, they would be the logical group to show an interest in worshiping the saint. Thus, it would be easy to develop a new patronate by bringing the students into a special relation of trust towards the Saint." No doubt, the students had Saint Nicholas held up to them as a shining example, even before they would think of adopting him as their patron saint. Once again, Meisen makes this clear:

"Where could they have found a better example than in Nicholas, who was praised not only as a perfect and diligent young man and student, but as an exceptional priest as well, a saint whose miracles at that time were echoed throughout the Western world. The students in these schools did not only hear of the deeds of Nicholas during classes, in sermons or lectures, but they also learned of his greatest miracles in the most literal sense of the words, 'at play.' The older students and their teachers were surely participants and actors in miracle plays that were performed on the eve of a saint's nameday, staged in honor of their patron. We can assume an especially close relationship of the students-actors in such miracle plays to the legends of Nicholas. In selecting material for plays concerning the saint of Myra, elements easily applied by the students, with which they could identify, are likely to have advanced adoption of the saint as patron of the ecclesiastical students.

"The Nicholas plays represent the oldest category of medieval miracle plays. When we also recall, on the basis of contemporary accounts, that the Saint Nicholas in these plays was not only presented with appropriately awe-inspiring personality traits, but also 'with a slight touch of humor,' then we can appreciate the atmosphere within which these plays were created."

Was this "slight touch of humor" the beginning of a European rehumanization of Saint Nicholas? Can we date the evolution of Santa Claus into his ho-ho-ho jolliness from the stage of a miracle play about Saint Nicholas in a twelfth-century church school in northern France? Not quite, I suppose. But the stage of a church school, with the saint being played by a teacher whose personal strengths and weaknesses would be known to members of the audience, as well as to fellow-members of the cast, is a relatively relaxed setting.

According to Meisen, Saint Nicholas emerged as patron saint of students "in response to the educational and instructional requirements of schooling" at that time. The patronate, begun in the convent schools, spread to the cathedral schools. The legend and the patronate illustrate how these things worked. Each patronate was often based on an earlier one. New legends might develop by combining elements in earlier ones, or by the addition of new anecdotal material. The student legend bolstered the student patronate. But both were Occidental, and they had no specific root in the Eastern tradition except for a remote link with stories of the young girls and a repetition of the three-theme.

The macabre quality of the student legend provided elements that the Middle Ages favored. The Greek tradition of Saint Nicholas had, by comparison, been too sedate, even when dealing with miracles. Moreover, the students needed a legend of their own. Sailors could cite many of Nicholas's rescues. Those who found themselves unjustly treated could point to the story of Emperor Constantine's three generals, but there was no student miracle. "It was therefore up to the gift of invention and combination among Western story tellers," Meisen writes, "to fill this gap and to create a narrative showing Nicholas specifically as the helper of students. Once such a story existed, medieval concepts acknowledged that there was now a concrete basis for a newly developed student patronate."

We encounter this type of development in the Saint Nicholas–Santa Claus image throughout its history. The church has always had difficulties with dramatic elements that are strongly rooted in folklore. The fairy tales of the Brothers Grimm were based on folkloric elements that had characteristics similar to miracle stories. The cannibalistic element in the student legend is just as crude as that in the story of Hansel and Gretel who are lost in the woods: the wicked witch tries to fatten up Hansel so that he will be good to eat. The Middle Ages, with their childlike cruelties, their executions as public spectacles, crusades that mixed ecstatic Christian idealism with greed and bigotry, glorious cathedrals and ravaging epidemics—they put their stamp on the Saint Nicholas cult, and they transformed the restrained, benevolent Bishop of Myra into a folk hero of the marketplace.

In miracle plays based on the student legend, Nicholas visits the butcher who has cut up the youngsters and put them into barrels—in the plays, the innkeeper image was later replaced by the more fearsome one of the butcher—and asks him for meat; or, in later versions, specifically for salted meat. Another metamorphosis occurs, in the thirteenth and fourteenth centuries, in the outward appearance of the students. In paintings and plays, they grow successively younger. Their hair is no longer shorn, monk-fashion; from young men and students they are transformed into little boys.

The resurrected victims became younger as the Saint Nicholas patronate began to extend to younger pupils and preschool children. Who, after all, stood more in need of protection in an uncertain and hostile world than the small and helpless child? This created a dilemma for painters using the theme of three young women whom Saint Nicholas helped with the money gifts. Obviously, if they had been in danger of being sold into slavery or prostitution because they lacked a dowry, they must have been sexually mature young women. Yet, as the patronate for children became more and more identified with Nicholas, painters felt constrained to envisage the three girls as childlike in appearance.

These paintings coincided with new artistic treatments of the student legend, including pictures that showed the saint as interceding for a group of children with the Virgin Mary. In Paris, a home for children was renamed "Hospitale pauperum scolarium, Sancti Nicolai de Lupera." In 1373, the seal of the home showed Saint Nicholas holding his right hand in blessing above a kneeling student. In Paris, too, Saint Nicholas's nameday, December 6, became a holiday for school children, who celebrated it with a torch parade.

Secular schools, established by major municipalities in Western Europe, followed church-directed educational institutions in adopting Nicholas as patron for their students. This pattern spread from France to England, Holland, Germany, and Denmark. In many cities, the first municipal schools were built close to churches dedicated to Saint Nicholas. The ecclesiastic and the secular began to separate, but schools retained and developed certain common denominators, the patronate of Saint Nicholas among them.

Histories, and particularly histories of saints, are always in danger of dehumanized dignity. The emergence of a jolly Santa Claus was forecast by a number of clues, quite aside from Western Europe's successful effort of turning a Byzantine bishop into the good-natured protector of little boys and girls. We have already seen that the saint slipped into becoming the patron, of all people, to pawnbrokers; and we will discover, in later chapters, that his protection was claimed by a wide variety of others.

But the legend of the traveling students had still another offshoot. Vagabondage was not restricted to scholarly voyagers in the mobile medieval society. Before long, other vagabonds appealed to Saint Nicholas for protection, including thieves and murderers. Such scum, in Shakespeare's time, was known as "Saint Nicholas clerks"—as we can see from *Henry IV,* part 1, act 2, scene 1:

> *Gadshill.* Sirrah, if they meet not with Saint Nicholas clerks, I'll give thee this neck.
> *Chamberlain.* No, I'll none of it . . . prithee, keep that for the hangman; for I know thou worshipp'st Saint Nicholas as truly as any man of falsehood many.

The universal appeal of a saint such as Nicholas is easy to understand. Where a humble student, or sailor, or marriageable young woman—or vagabond and crook—might hesitate to call upon more remote figures in the religious hierarchy in moments of fear and stress, a more human image could be addressed without hesitation. And Saint Nicholas, by the end of the Middle Ages, was becoming more and more human to wider and wider segments of the European population.

"Saint Nicholas Resuscitating Three Youths" is the name of this painting by Lorenzo di Bicci. It forms the panel from the predella of an altarpiece prepared for the Monastery of San Niccolò in Florence. Dressed in his bishop's robes, with mitre, the saint is shown with a halo as he blesses the three young men he has brought back to life. The man and woman kneeling in the foreground may be considered as being their parents, although the legend does not speak of the three youths as being brothers. *The Metropolitan Museum of Art, New York. Gift of Francis Kleinberger, 1916*

North European woodcut, from the Middle Ages, showing the saint as he reconstitutes the three students dismembered by the innkeeper. He is wearing his bishop's robes and carrying a mitre.

This is a rare recreation of the resuscitation of the three dismembered students, as it shows them stepping out of the barrels in which they had been kept. They appear as full-grown young men, rather than as children. The painting, by Francesco Pesellino, is at the Galleria Buonarroti, Florence. *Alinari*

Representation of the saint by a painter of the Lombard School, fourteenth century, from the collection of San Francesco, Lodi. *Frick Art Reference Library, New York*

6. NEARLY EVERYBODY'S SAINT

This painting of Saint Nicholas, by Bartholomäus Zeitblom, is unique in that it shows the saint contemplating the three balls that have become symbolic of his work, dating back to the legend of the three bags of gold with which he helped three young women obtain their dowries. *Collections of the Governing Prince of Liechtenstein, Vaduz*

You are mingling with a festive, excitedly chattering crowd in a provincial French or Italian town. The year is, let us say, 1236; the date, December 5. It is late afternoon. All around the marketplace are food vendors. There has been some drinking in the city's taverns. By now, some of the men are as unruly as the children that are part of the throng moving toward the central marketplace. There will be something new to see and hear before the sun goes down: a play about a miraculous picture of Saint Nicholas.

It is a lively, at times raucous play, involving invaders, bandits, robbery, and violence. But in the end, Christian virtue wins out, and the villains turn honest, contrite, and faithful. The play was probably conceived as a pious but dramatic legend by someone who lived in what is today the Italian region of Calabria when it was part of the Byzantine Empire.

The villain of the play is a Vandal chieftain, Barbarus. In our language, *vandalism* stands for mindless destruction. This meaning has come down to us from the time the Vandals, a Teutonic tribe, settled in North Africa and crossed the Mediterranean on piratical expeditions during the sixth century. This particular Vandal chieftain has looted many towns in Calabria and taken local citizens prisoners. He is worried that his treasures might, in turn, be taken from him by dubious friends or open foes.

Barbarus is told that one of his looted treasures is a magical portrait of Saint Nicholas. He learns from a prisoner that the picture, or icon, will guarantee luck and wealth to its owner, as long as it remains in his possession. Barbarus is, of course, delighted to hear this good news. He assumes that the icon will transfer its strength to any possessor, whether ownership is legitimate or by robbery.

Greedy, simple-minded Barbarus, portrayed on the stage as a cunning boor who is partly fearsome and partly ridiculous, decides to turn the holy icon into a magical watch dog for his accumulated loot. But while Barbarus goes off to celebrate his now-safeguarded gains, his loot in turn is looted.

The audience in the marketplace roars with laughter as the boorish, drunken chieftain displays shock, confusion, and anger when he discovers that most of his treasure has disappeared. But the Saint Nicholas icon is still there. Barbarus, who only knows violent punishment, decides to treat Saint Nicholas as he would one of his own soldiers who may fail in guard duty: he threatens to give him a good thrashing unless he sees to it, miraculous or otherwise, that the ill-gotten treasures are returned.

If you see yourself as a member of the audience, you can feel its excitement as the plot thickens: the holy icon has taken on human, indeed superhuman, characteristics; it is like an actor on the stage. Can Saint Nicholas permit his holy image to be mistreated, cursed, "beaten," damaged in demeaning ways by the piratical unbeliever?

Now the scene changes. The bandits are assembled. With much shouting and arguing, they are about to divide the remaining loot among themselves. But just as they are about to lay hands on the loot, Saint Nicholas appears before them as a vivid apparition. Angered, he subdues them with his magnificence. He threatens to take them all before the town's judges unless they immediately return all stolen goods to their rightful owners. His appearance sobers and frightens the thieves. If they do not obey him, Nicholas threatens, they will all wind up with a rope around their necks. The thieves, contrite, return the loot.

But Barbarus is even more deeply impressed. In the closing scene of the play, the Vandal invader kisses the icon of the saint. On his return to North Africa, he sees to it that all members of his household become Christians. Finally, he builds a chapel dedicated to the holy man whose apparition forced him to change his ways. And that, the stage play states in closing, is how Saint Nicholas became famous even in Africa.

There is a wickedly impious note in this play, in line with the raucous nature of other public dramas of the period. The very idea that an icon of the saint could be threatened with a beating is hardly in line with the traditional awe that surrounds the stories, paintings, and plays that have Saint Nicholas as a central character. True, the "happy ending" makes everything all right and furnishes an excuse for some of the rowdyism in the first two-thirds of the play. Violence, with some sort of "redeeming social value"—to use a contemporary expression—was as much a part of the late Middle Ages as it had been in antiquity and remains in today's motion picture and television shows, not to mention the miracle-cum-morality play's successors on our own theatrical stages.

A similar story, dealing with a Jew unjustly accused by a Christian, includes a dramatic device showing considerable stage wisdom and plot sophistication. It has the same kind of happy ending as the play featuring the threatened icon. The story tells of a Christian who finds himself in debt and persuades a Jewish friend to make him a loan. Lacking collateral, he swears by the icon of Saint Nicholas that he will return the borrowed sum promptly, on a fixed date. The date for repayment comes around. The Christian borrower now has the money to repay his creditor, but he just does not want to live up to his promise. Faced with the Jewish lender's request for payment, the borrower swears that he owes him nothing. Apparently banking on a Jew's delicate standing within Christian society at that time, the borrower takes the case to court, confident that he can convince the judge that he is being unjustly accused.

The clever twist within the story is the shrewd Christian's device of making sure that, technically, he does place the money in his creditor's hand. To do this, he hollows out a stick he carries with him. And before he declares under oath that he has given the borrowed sum back to the Jew, he manages to maneuver the creditor into holding the stick for a moment. The Jew, quite naturally, is angry when the court declares him to be in the wrong; he leaves the courtroom with a slighting remark about Saint Nicholas, in whose name the Christian borrower had promised prompt repayment.

But Saint Nicholas is not to be trifled with. When the crooked borrower is on his way home, elated by his trick and victory, an irresistible fatigue overcomes him. He is forced to lie down on the road. No one can rouse him from his deep sleep or trance. Lying in the middle of the highway, the crooked debtor is run over by a rapidly approaching horse and wagon. He suffers a painful death. Moreover, the wagon's wheels have run over the hollow stick, break it and spill the borrowed money onto the road, thus exposing the ingenious but wicked trick.

The Jewish friend is called to the scene of the accident; the judge also joins the group to discuss the duplicity of the borrower. As Saint Nicholas had been invoked during the transaction, all participants feel that the saint has had a role in setting matters right in this dramatic manner. The Jew acknowledges that the money inside the broken walking stick is the exact amount borrowed from him, but he refuses to accept it while his one-time friend is lying lifeless, broken in body, in the middle of the road.

If Saint Nicholas is powerful enough to take a human life to expose a fraudulent financial claim, the Jewish creditor suggests, he should be able to bring his one-time friend back to life. The saint, apparently convinced by this argument, acts quickly. Hardly has the creditor expressed his humane and generous thoughts when the Christian comes back to life, his wounds erased. He stands up and walks as if nothing has happened. The Jew, convinced by the miracle, has himself and his family converted to the Christian faith.

Like so many Western European legends of Saint Nicholas this one developed during the twelfth century. The story was retold in many hymns in praise of Saint Nicholas that gained popularity in the thirteenth, fourteenth, and fifteenth centuries in England, France, and Germany.

Four scenes based on this legend appear in the stained-glass windows of Chartres Cathedral. The first shows the Jew as he hands the money over to the Christian, who lifts his hand in solemn oath before a statue of Saint Nicholas. Next, the Christian is shown handing his hollowed-out stick to his creditor. On the third window panel, a cart pulled by two oxen crushes the sleeping Christian and breaks his walking stick from which gold coins roll into the street. And finally, the Jew is baptized in the presence of two priests.

This legend shows Saint Nicholas as the guarantor of a solemn oath taken in his name, a practice later used in many different ways. Knights preparing for combat took an oath to the saint; crusaders pledged that they would proceed without rest or delay; in Holland, the phrase, "I swear by Nicholas the Saint . . ." became almost commonplace.

The curious role of Saint Nicholas as patron of pawnbrokers developed directly from these practices. The legend of the debtor dramatized the saint's role as a protector of financial integrity, as guardian of commitments made in good faith. The international banking community, which grew from the activities of merchants in Florence during the twelfth and thirteenth centuries, was based on an ethic of mutual trust. Mr. Harry Harlem, secretary of the Pawnbrokers Association of New York City, notes that the three golden balls were part of the coat of arms of the Medici; Giovanni di Bicci dei Medici established the Medici European trading and banking empire, with its center in Florence. Meisen, with a touch of irony, explains the link between the moneylenders and their secular temples to Saint Nicholas as follows:

"The ancient heraldric sign of the Medici had been three golden balls. As Saint Nicholas had, traditionally, been identified in Italy with three golden balls, recalling the three moneybags he used to save three young women from disgrace —in France, he is usually shown with the three students as they emerge from a barrel—a link between the symbols of Nicholas and the heraldic sign of this well-known banking family did not seem far-fetched. The period as a whole turned toward the saint in commercial transactions with particular confidence.

"That it should have been the Medici, above all, who chose the symbol of Saint Nicholas as their own heraldic sign may have been due to the fact that Florence, their seat, played a particularly significant role in the history of the Nicholas cult. Once the other Florentine and Lombardic merchants, as involved in monetary dealings as the Medici, adopted the three balls, they quickly came to symbolize the whole profession. When the Italian bankers opened branches abroad, the professional symbol spread to the rest of the European West." R. Chambers, in *The Book of Days II* (London, 1863), also links the three balls or moneybags with Saint Nicholas's gift to the three young women. From England, the triple symbol made its way to the United States, and while it is not to be found on Wall Street, tradition-minded pawnbrokers still display it outside their shops.

All this shows the increasing practicality with which devout Western European Christians viewed the miraculous powers of Saint Nicholas. Dowries for needy girls, ships in distress, and grain shortages might have been centers of tragedy and disasters in an earlier age, far away, in the Eastern Mediterranean. By now, nearly a thousand years had passed. The world was still a dangerous and unpredictable place. Emotional and, indeed, material needs had spread far beyond those of the simple sailors, soldiers, and townsfolk in and around Myra.

As the Middle Ages began to yield to the Renaissance, to a new, inspiring link-up with ancient Greece, not just the Greek-controlled Byzantine Empire and its Roman successor, Saint

Nicholas seemed about to become Everybody's Favorite Saint. If yearning virgins, barren wives, helpless infants, thieves and financiers, traveling students and pirating Vandals could pledge allegiance to Saint Nicholas, where would it all end?

It ended, as we know, with Santa Claus. But not yet.

Stained-glass window, Cathedral at Bourges, France, with a series of scenes showing miracles of Saint Nicholas.

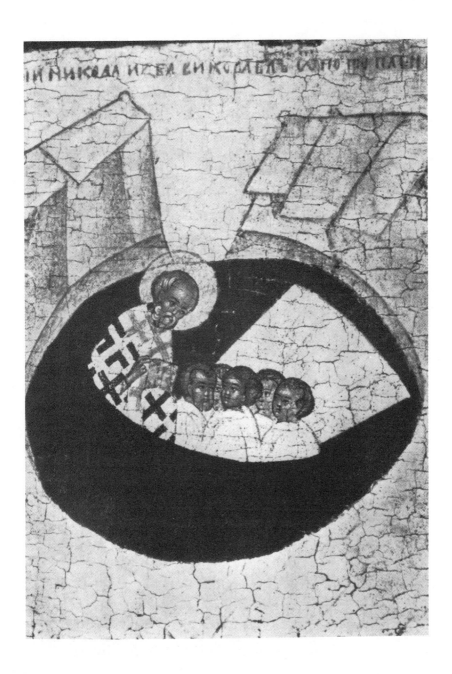

Border scenes of a fifteenth-century Russian icon, depicting the life of the saint, include this stylized conception of Saint Nicholas and sailors in a boat. *The Russian Museum, Leningrad*

Saint Nicholas, exorcizing a kneeling man, with the Devil escaping from the man's mouth. This is one scene from the border of a larger icon devoted to the saint's miracles, from the Cathedral of St. John the Theologian at Kolomna, painted in the fourteenth century. *Tretyakov Gallery, Moscow*

A jeweled reliquary box stands inside a niche of the main chapel of Saint Nicholas Greek Orthodox Church of Flushing, just outside New York City. The church is part of a vibrant, modern community. Pieces of Saint Nicholas's skull, garments, and coffin, together with a vial of myrrh, rest inside the relic box. Within a few hundred feet from the buzzing twentieth-century traffic on 196th Street and Northern Boulevard, these relics symbolize the migration of the saint's image and influence during different eras and in many geographic directions.

In the tenth century, the cult of Saint Nicholas migrated into the Slavic East of Europe, by way of Kiev.

A hundred years later, in the eleventh century, the saint's cultural journey into Western Europe began by way of Bari, now in southern Italy.

In the nineteenth century, the saint's image was transformed into Santa Claus, in the state of New York, as we shall see in the next chapter.

And in the twentieth century, relics of the saint arrived at the Saint Nicholas church in Flushing as part of an ecumenical gift from Bari.

When Christianity came to the Slavic peoples, Kiev was a city-state populated by the Rhôs and Slavs. This sovereign city had made several unsuccessful military attacks in the direction of Constantinople in the ninth century. The Rhôs had adopted Christianity to some degree, but the movement was set back by the invasion of northern tribes. The Christian faith was revived by Prince Oleg and his wife, Olga. In 911, Oleg signed a treaty of friendship with the Byzantine rulers; Emperor Leo sent precious gifts and relics from Constantinople, among them relics of Saint Nicholas.

After Oleg died, his widow, Olga, traveled to Constantinople to be baptized in the capital city of Christianity. But even while she was still making arrangements for the arrival of a Christian bishop in Constantinople, she was deposed by her son, who preferred Islam to Christianity. He was, however, defeated during an attack on Byzantine forces and died in Kiev.

Olga's grandson, Vladimir, fully opened the doors to the

Christian faith among the Slavs. As prince of Kiev, Vladimir sent Byzantine Emperor Basil II an army of six thousand men that enabled the emperor to crush the rebellion of a rival. As a prize for supplying these troops, Vladimir asked the emperor to give him an imperial princess for a wife. But Basil was in no hurry to comply with this request. The impatient Vladimir thereupon invaded Byzantine territory in the Crimea, occupying the town of Cherson. The emperor hastily sent his sister, Anna, to Cherson to appease his aggressive ally.

As Anna was a daughter of Emperor Romanus II, thus definitely "born to the purple," Vladimir was satisfied. He had himself baptized in Cherson (either in 988 or 989) by his own bishop but in the presence of a Greek priest who had accompanied Anna from Constantinople. Following his baptism, the marriage ceremony was performed, and Valdimir returned the town of Cherson to his new brother-in-law, the emperor, as a present.

Vladimir's Christian marriage was a crucial factor in the spread of Saint Nicholas worship. Vladimir was determined to demonstrate to his new bride that he was a thoroughgoing Christian. He did so with characteristic enthusiasm. If contemporary chroniclers did not exaggerate (and they probably did), the prince of Kiev gave up five wives and eight hundred concubines when he married Anna. To prove his loyalty beyond doubt, Vladimir ordered the statue of Perun, supreme deity of the Slavs, "tied to a horse's tail and dragged down to the Dnieper River." There, twelve men beat the statue with sticks to "chastise" the "demon who had deceived men in this guise." The idol was then tossed into the river.

Prince Vladimir next ordered the wholesale baptism of the people of Kiev. They were assembled at the riverbank, then walked into the Dnieper, where they were baptized in a mass ceremony. Princess Anna, who viewed most of this drama with a good deal of disdain, was repelled rather than attracted by her husband's methods. She complained of Vladimir's crude habits to her cousin, the Empress Theophano, who lived in Rome. As Theophano's own marriage to Emperor Otto II had also been arranged as a deal in Byzantine imperial politics, she sympathized with her cousin's fate, stranded as she was among the nouveaux Christians of Kiev. Replying to her letter, the widowed empress sent Anna a note of sympathy and encouragement, together with relics of Saint Nicholas and other saints.

Having moved northward to Kiev in the tenth century, the Saint Nicholas cult traveled to the West in a still more picturesque manner: one hundred years later, the saint's body was taken from its tomb in Myra and transported to Bari. There had been several earlier plots to kidnap the saint's remains to the western part of the crumbling empire. The ultimately successful removal took place in 1087; the ship carrying the remains arrived in the port of Bari on May 9.

To this day, the city of Bari recalls this event with an annual celebration. A flag-bedecked fishing fleet takes a symbolic coffin out to sea and then returns to the port for festivities that are both folkloric and religious. It is not clear whether the eleventh-century removal of the saint was carried out by a merchant ship, possibly armed, or whether Bari soldiers landed near Myra, entered the town, overpowered the tomb's guards, broke into the sarcophagus, and brought the remains to their native city. In retrospect, the transfer of Saint Nicholas's body has been interpreted as a pious act, designed to forestall any harm that might come to the remains from Moslem invaders. Still, more far-reaching socioreligious and historical trends were reflected in this event than a mere gain by Bari over Myra.

During the Middle Ages, Bari, established during the fourth century, was a departure point for pilgrims traveling to holy places in the East, including Jerusalem and Myra. The patronate of Saint Nicholas over sailors and fishermen, and the legends of his feats in their safety and rescue, made the saint a popular figure among Bari's sailors and merchants; they had come to regard him as one of theirs. At the same time, the Byzantine part of the empire was losing temporal and spiritual power. Its treasures became spoils to soldiers of fortune, pirates, religious fanatics, and plain brigands. Thus, the transfer of Saint Nicholas's remains may well have been a combination of contrasting and overlapping motivations.

Bari was too far removed from Rome at that time to be under effective control of the popes; their rule, too, reflected transition and turmoil within the empire. Bari became a bishopric under Byzantine control in the tenth century, but in 1025 it was recognized as a metropolitan see by Pope John XIX and in 1069 by Pope Alexander II. The papal hold on Bari was tenuous. It seems fair to assume that the transfer of Saint Nicholas's body was a local Bari enterprise, not initiated by the papacy, and possibly even a cause of irritation in Rome.

But soon after the saint's remains were deposited in Bari, they became a center of prestige, pilgrimage, and local pride. Until an appropriate resting place had been established, the saint's remains were kept hidden in the catacombs of a Bari monastery. Two years after the arrival of the remains, in 1089, Archbishop Elias of Bari was appointed to his post by Pope Urban II, and his main task was the building of a magnificent basilica for Saint Nicholas. The basilica, completed in 1108, is one of the most impressive edifices in Christendom. The building was extended and restored several times, but its key elements have remained intact. The interior is divided into three naves by columns, with galleries above the aisles. The basilica's facade has retained its original grandeur.

Part of the building crews were Moslem workmen from the Near East or North Africa. Being skilled craftsmen as well as pious followers of Islam, they incorporated Arabic calligraphy into a design which read, "There is no God but Allah, and Mohammed is His Prophet." When church officials realized, several years later, what the message said, they decided to leave the beauty of it intact and refrained from removing the inscription.

While Bari celebrates the saint's arrival in its port each May 9, it virtually ignores other dates connected with Saint Nicholas, including any relation to Christmas, gift-giving, and children. The children of Bari, like boys and girls throughout Italy, hang up their stockings for gifts on January 6, the eve of Epiphany. The religio-folkloric practice is that children expect gifts from a benign witch, known as Befana. Her name is an obvious adaptation of the word *Epiphany*. The witch's original identity is lost in folk traditions that doubtlessly predate Christianity. Even in Bari, Befana is the successful rival of Santa Claus. Her role, somewhat in the manner of Santa Claus—who knows who was "naughty or nice"—is ambivalent. Her involvement with children is said to date back to the birth of Christ when she missed seeing the Three Wise Men and was condemned to search for them forever. Also, benign or not, for generations Italian mothers have used the Befana's name to frighten their children.

While the cult of Saint Nicholas in Western Europe gained its major impetus with the arrival of the saint's body in Bari, the attitude of the church of Rome has fluctuated. This was illustrated when the Vatican's universal calendar for 1970 listed December 6 as the Second Sunday of Advent, but did not mention the saint's name. This started a minor, although worldwide, furor. The *New York Times* carried a dispatch under the heading "Santa Is Saying Good-by As Major Catholic Saint." The report, by the Reuters News Agency from Rome, and dated December 24, 1969, stated: "Santa Claus is having his last Christmas this year as a major Roman Catholic saint. When the new Catholic calendar comes into force January 1, Santa—St. Nicholas of Bari—will be relegated from obligatory to voluntary veneration for the world's 700 million Roman Catholics."

Reports of this type created a good deal of confusion. In answer to hundreds of questions, Father Badia, writing in the *Liguorian Sunday Bulletin* of Liguori, Missouri, says, "No, Saint Nick has not been banned." He explains that the saint had only been "displaced from the universal calendar of the saints and relegated to local devotion." He quotes the Vatican newspaper *Osservatore Romano* and the Reverend Annibale Bugnini, secretary of the newly created Congregation for Divine Worship, as answering the question, Where have the saints gone? by saying, "They go back to the Roman Mythology where they were taken from years ago at different phases of Christian piety."

Naturally, no matter how politely and theologically put, devotees of Saint Nicholas regarded this change as downgrading. The Dominican Fathers who administer the Basilica of Saint Nicholas in Bari were particularly upset by the ruling. The Saint Nicholas expert of the Dominican order, Father Damiano Bova, undertook a research project designed to prove that the saint was worthy of universal veneration and a true miracle worker. Father Damiano says, "I hope our evidence will reopen the case of Saint Nicholas before the Vatican Commission and get him reinstated in the Church calendar. But, meanwhile, what is most important is that the cult of Saint Nicholas is alive—not just in Bari—but throughout the world, to this very day." Since the Vatican ruling, no discernible difference has occurred in veneration of the saint in the countries where many churches bear the name of Saint Nicholas, or where his patronates have been a matter of long and popular tradition.

It was about the time of the change in the Vatican's value judgment on Saint Nicholas that Greek Orthodox Archbishop Iakovos suggested to Pope Paul VI that relics from Bari might be transferred to the United States. The gift was subsequently made as a "sign of the growing rapprochement and affection developing between the two ancient churches which were united for ten centuries." While some of the relics were retained at the Greek Orthodox Cathedral in New York City, the greater part were transferred to the Shrine of Saint Nicholas in Flushing and deposited there on December 5, 1972. The relics were presented to Archbishop Iakovos by Roman Catholic Bishop Francis Mugavero of Brooklyn. During vespers, an intercessory service was offered on behalf of the maritime world, in recognition of the saint's ancient patronage of seafaring men. Representatives of the Greek shipping community and of seamen's associations were also present. Among those participating in the ecumenical proceedings was the Right Reverend Richard B. Martin, Auxiliary Bishop of the Episcopal Diocese of Long Island.

The following day, December 6, the feast day of the saint, a Hieratical Divine Liturgy was celebrated at the church, conducted by His Grace Philoteas, Titular Bishop of Meloa, assisted by the pastor of the Church of Saint Nicholas, the Reverend Constantine E. Volaitis. With the relics of the saint present, and with his church very much a living, bustling establishment in twentieth-century Greater New York, Father Volaitis has emphasized that "Saint Nicholas teaches us that our needs in this age are as real and as poignant as they were when he was among us; that man's fundamental hopes and fears have essentially remained the same; that the need for loving and being loved is not altered."

The presence of the remains of Saint Nicholas, Father Volaitis says, "provides a sense of personal intimacy between the saint and the members of the congregation. It has definitely heightened the spiritual strength of our parish: we are like a family, and, in a very special sense, we feel that the saint is among us. We do not know, of course, whether the often-reported healing powers or other miraculous gifts of the saint will begin to play a role in our parish; right now, we are simply very happy indeed that he is among us."

This icon, from the famous Novodevichy (New Maidens') Monastery within Moscow's Kremlin complex, dates to the twelfth century. The icon may originally have come from Novgorod, for centuries distinguished for its church art. *Tretyakov Gallery, Moscow*

Icon of Saint Nicholas on wood, seventeenth century. *Byzantine Museum, Athens*

The full-length painting of Saint Nicholas, attributed to Titian (Tiziano Vecelli), shows the symbolic three balls at his left foot. Church of San Niccolò, Venice. *Anderson-Alinari*

This stone relief at the Basilica of Saint Nicholas, Bari, shows the saint surrounded by sculpted versions of key events in his life and legends.

The graphic transition from Saint Nicholas to Santa Claus is shown in the nineteenth-century Dutch painting by J. Schenkman. The picture, entitled "Saint Nicholas and His Servant," shows the saint in bishop's robes, with mitre, astride a horse. Later paintings added one reindeer, rather than a horse, pulling a sled. *The New-York Historical Society*

8. NEW YORK'S UNIVERSAL SANTA CLAUS

The New-York Historical Society issued a broadside devoted to Saint Nicholas in 1810, at a time when such leading members of the Society as John Pintard emphasized New York City's historical links with the saint as part of the city's Dutch heritage. The woodcut was executed by Alexander Anderson (1775–1870). The beehive behind the saint presumably symbolizes diligence and thrift, the dog, loyalty. The two children on the upper right may represent a "nice" girl who has gathered up gifts, including a doll, and a "naughty" boy with a twig or switch sticking up through a buttonhole, resembling the one in the saint's right hand. Below is a fireplace with gifts inside the stocking on the left and a switch on the right. *The New-York Historical Society*

Santa Claus, as we know him today, is a creation of the city and state of New York. His dress, manner of travel, reindeer, sled, and North Pole habitat are not the accumulation of Nordic folklore or other European traditions but the work of New York artists. Nor did Santa Claus arrive, full-blown, as patron saint of the city of Amsterdam, brought to the New World by the Dutch settlers who established New Amsterdam.

For the most part, there is no arguing with legends, including those highlighting the history of Saint Nicholas worship from the Dark through the Middle Ages and into the Renaissance. But the legend of a reindeer-powered *Sinta Claes* who, as it were, accompanied the Dutch settlers in the early years of the seventeenth century to the island of Manhattan, and has lived here happily ever after, needs correction.

True enough, Saint Nicholas crossed the Atlantic with the explorers, militant sailors and merchants who sought their fortune in the New World. As the traditional patron saint of seamen, Saint Nicholas was dear to these transatlantic seafarers. As the Vikings may have been the first to land in the New World, it is worth remembering that they dedicated a cathedral in Greenland to the saint. Christopher Columbus, when he landed on Haiti during his first voyage, named a port after Saint Nicholas. And what is now the city of Jacksonville, Florida, was originally named, by Spanish explorers, Saint Nicholas Ferry.

The Protestant Reformation in Europe had in some countries sought to eliminate the veneration of saints, but Saint Nicholas survived. Specifically, in what are now North Germany and Holland, Saint Nicholas as a folkloric image—although based on religious tradition—emerged from the concept of the saint as a purely ecclesiastical figure. That is one reason for the many local pseudonyms: Father Christmas in England, *Weihnachts-mann* in Germany, *Père Noel* in France, Kris Kringle (which is derived from the German *Christ-Kindlein*, or Christ Child) among the Pennsylvania Dutch.

In Holland, at any rate, *Sinta Claes* survived the Reformation unharmed. The *Catholic Encyclopedia* states that "the Dutch puritans of New Amsterdam" had "disguised the popish saint as

a nordic magician." Yet, the link between the Santa Claus custom and Nordic traditions is speculative. One authority, George
H. McKnight, has stated: "In the practices associated in our
time with the name Santa Claus we have survivals of pagan
sacred custom once regarded as important in the furtherance
of human welfare. Perhaps influenced superficially by the Ger-
manic gods, eventually they came to be connected with the
honor of the Christian saints. They afford a remarkable illustra-
tion of the longevity of folk customs. With meaning lost or
changed, the older forms persist."

Over and over, the Nordic god Odin (or: Othin, Woden, Wo-
dan, Wotan, Wuotan) is named by historians as the image after
which Saint Nicholas is supposed to have been modeled. But
Saint Nicholas never took a hold in Scandinavia until fairly
recently; when a picture of Santa Claus appeared on a Danish
Christmas seal, issued by a children's welfare organization in
1958, one clergyman, Reverend Paul Nedergaard, denounced
it and said, "These seals bear a symbol of a pagan goblin." No
one paid much attention to it by then. Meisen denies that the
cult of the saint can be "traced back to the Germanic-pagan
period." He insists that it moved from the ecclesiastical arena
by way of convent-educated students, into folkways associated
with children.

What was the Santa Claus, then, who crossed the ocean with
the Dutch settlers of New Amsterdam?

Scholars differ. Writing in the *New-York Historical Society
Quarterly* (October 1954), Dr. Charles W. Jones takes issue with
what he regards as "a legend which is repeated yearly in those
Christmas books which blossom with the poinsettias," a legend
which "has been essentially static for a century" and is "most
clearly stated" in Mary L. Booth's *History of the City of New
York*, a book published in 1859, as follows:

"The Dutch had five national festivals which were observed
throughout the city; namely, Kerstrydt (Christmas); Nieuw jar
(New Year); Paas (the Passover); Pinxter (Whitsuntide); and
Santa Claus (St. Nicholas or Christ-kinkle day). . . . But Santa
Claus day was the best of all in the estimation of the little folks,
who, of all others, enjoy holidays the most intensely. It is notable, too, for having been the day sacred to St. Nicholas, the
patron saint of New York, who presided at the figure-head of
the first emigrant ship that touched her shores, who gave his

name to the first church erected within her walls, and who has ever since been regarded as having special charge of the destinies of his favorite city.

"To the children, he was a jolly, rosy-cheeked little old man, with a low-crowned hat, a pair of flemish trunk-hose and a pipe of immense length, who drove his reindeer sleigh loaded with gifts from the frozen regions of the North over the roofs of New Amsterdam for the benefit of good children. Models of propriety were they for a week preceding the eventful Christmas Eve. When it came, they hung their stockings, carefully labelled, that the Saint might make no mistakes, in the chimney corner, and went early to bed, chanting the Santa Claus hymn in addition to their usual devotions."

Dr. Jones writes that "everyone repeats this story," including Mrs. Schuyler Van Rensselaer in her *History of New York City in the Seventeenth Century* and I. N. Phelps Stokes in *Iconography of Manhattan Island*. He cites an Amsterdam ordinance, reflecting Reformation sentiment, directed against "superstition and fables of the papacy," that there were to be no gatherings on Saint Nicholas Eve, and no selling of "candy, eatables and other merchandise." Jones says that "the very presence of such laws shows that St. Nicholas was lurking underground." DeGroot, whose work I have cited earlier in this volume, also states that such ordinances were ineffective. Dr. Jones next puts the question, "But if the citizens of New Netherland had defied the laws of their country by giving aid and solace to the enemy, wouldn't some record of the treason appear? None is known."

The historian had "not found evidence of St. Nicholas in any form—in juveniles or periodicals or diaries—in the period of Dutch rule, or straight through the seventeenth and eighteenth centuries to the year 1773." Jones adds that the first evidence is an item in *Rivington's Gazetteer* (December 23, 1773): "Last Monday, the anniversary of St. Nicholas, otherwise called Santa Claus, was celebrated at Protestant Hall, at Mr. Waldron's; where a great number of sons of the ancient saint celebrated the day with great joy and festivity." Another such notice appeared in 1774. There was no further mention until 1793, long after the Revolutionary War, which had changed the social patterns of New York City quite thoroughly.

Now, then, who is right and who is wrong? Mrs. Booth with her colorful description of a Dutch Santa Claus in New Amsterdam, or Dr. Jones's fruitless search for evidence to support such a report?

Probably Dr. Jones. Because even members of the New-York Historical Society who all regard Santa Claus as an early Dutch pioneer have to limit themselves to describing post-Revolutionary customs, a sort of Santa Renaissance that was no longer Dutch, definitely American, and possibly anti-British. Mixed into this picture is the social and political division of New York City's population. For example: while there was a group referring to itself as the Sons of Saint Nicholas (as the 1773 newspaper report showed), there also existed a Society of Saint Andrew and, believe it or not, the "Sons of Saint Tammany."

In our own days, the term *Tammany Hall* has been associated with tough and unscrupulous political manipulators within the Democratic party's "machine" in New York City. But its origin is quite different. As everybody knows, the Dutch landed on Manhattan Island in 1611, which was purchased in 1626 from the Indians for the equivalent of the famous twenty-four dollars. When the territory was transferred to English control, in 1664, the population was about ten thousand. During the pre-Revolutionary period, the societies that emphasized loyalty to the British crown were those named after Saint Andrew, Saint George, and Saint David. The revolutionists, combining a sense of humor with emphasis on native Americanism, formed an association named after Tammanend, a Delaware Indian chief, and that is how the "Sons of Saint Tammany" got their name.

Against this background, let us see what Dr. Jones, the cynical realist, has to say about the development of the Sons of Saint Nicholas. First of all, Jones recalls: "St. Nicholas in the eighteenth century was no longer anathema to reformers, as he had been in the seventeenth century. Even before the end of the seventeenth century, Jan Steen and other northern painters were creating their lovable scenes of St. Nicholas Eve. Unlike England, the Continent had learned to tolerate its children's idol." Jones adds:

"There is no evidence that St. Nicholas suggested Holland to the New York patriots; for a century, ever since the Whig revolt in England, Holland was increasingly cut off from the Colonies, and as Hanover replaced Orange on the English throne, the Dutch, if noticed at all, were not noticed with favor. When New Yorkers resurrected St. Nicholas, they did so because he was anti-British, not because he was pro-Dutch, and he was not to be taken seriously."

The cautious Dr. Jones concludes that "we can assert with surety that the New York patriots formed a local society and dedicated it to St. Nicholas as a New York symbol," whereby they "never had Holland in mind at all."

The man who put Saint Nicholas on the map in New York, after that, was John Pintard, who founded the New-York Historical Society and was active in many other organizations. Pintard included Saint Nicholas in his private almanac in 1793. As he helped to create Washington's Birthday and the Fourth of July as national holidays, Jones believes that Pintard "was thinking of St. Nicholas and Nicholas Day in the same patriotic spirit and would push the cult for the same patriotic reasons." Jones wrote that, to Pintard, "St. Nicholas had become the patron saint of his city," and he probably "found it very easy to associate St. Nicholas with the Dutch" because by then the establishment of New Amsterdam had become associated with civic pride.

With Pintard at the helm, the New-York Historical Society held its first anniversary dinner for Saint Nicholas in 1810. We are now rapidly approaching the moment of the Great Saint Nicholas Renaissance in New York! Alexander Anderson's woodcut of Saint Nicholas, which is reproduced on these pages, was commissioned by Pintard. The symbolism of the beehive and the dog, sitting on his hind legs, can only be guessed; perhaps Anderson was simply seeking to illustrate diligence and watchfulness. On January 10, 1809, Dr. David Hosack said at the society's annual banquet, while delivering a toast, "To the memory of St. Nicholas. May the virtuous habits and simple manners of our Dutch ancestors be not lost in the luxuries and refinements of the present time." At this same dinner, Washington Irving was nominated for membership in the society.

Aside from the mercurial, imaginative Pintard, three men created the modern image of Santa Claus:

Washington Irving (1783–1859), who combined scholarship with wit, was a traveler in much of Europe but helped give the young American nation a literary identity. He was only in his early twenties when he concocted *Diedrich Knickerbocker's A History of New York from the Beginning of the World to the End of the Dutch Dynasty.* He had started it off as a spoof of the pompous historical writings of one Dr. Samuel L. Mitchell. But the idea proliferated like a jungle growth, as Irving's imagination mixed history with spoofery—until no one could be sure what was fact and what was satirical fancy.

Clement Clarke Moore (1779–1863), a leading Hebrew scholar, was instrumental in establishing the General Theological Seminary. At Christmastime in 1822 he wrote "A Visit from St. Nicholas." The basic theme and indeed some of the phrasing are obviously modeled after Irving's imaginings. If Washington Irving created a nineteenth-century *Vita* of Saint Nicholas-Santa Claus, Moore created the memorable cadences, the phrases that became so ingrained, the images so vivid, strong, and seemingly rooted in a long tradition, that he brought Santa Claus to life for the present day and, with modern communications, the whole world.

Thomas Nast (1840–1902) was a German-born illustrator with such a natural gift for satiric line drawings that he joined the staff of *Harper's Weekly* at the age of eighteen. While Irving's imaginative writings provided a pseudo-history of a Dutch Santa Claus in post-Revolutionary American social life, Nast's black-and-white drawings added an indelible visual dimension.

Dr. Neils H. Sonne, librarian of the General Theological Seminary, New York, confirmed Moore's authorship of his influential poem in a paper, " 'The Night Before Christmas': Who Wrote It?" which appeared in *The Historical Magazine* of the Protestant Episcopal Church (Vol. XLI, No. 4). Dr. Sonne also says that "Moore provided the word imagery" that numerous illustrators attempted to portray; but it was Nast, nearly half a century later, who "did so in a manner that has become standardized and typical."

The impact of these three men is still with us. Moore, in particular, had the common touch that comes with the childlike sincerity of a learned man; you say to yourself, " 'Twas the night before Christmas . . ." and Clement Moore's plain and rhythmic words begin to follow one another in your memory. The Nast cartoons on these pages speak for themselves. But what were Irving's particular contributions? Jones says that "without Irving there would be no Santa Claus." His imaginary *History* contains twenty-five references to the popular saint. It has it all: from the immigrant ship *Goede Vrouw* (Good Woman), to a figurehead of Santa Claus on its prow. He gives "detailed" accounts of the alleged early Dutch festivities in New Amsterdam, gamboling children, cookies for sale, establishment of a church dedicated to the saint.

The prolific Irving's modern legend had what the traditional *Vitae* lacked: color, detail, and a robustness that seemed as true as life itself. Where the original *Vita* writers were concerned with brief tales of virtue and superhuman saintliness, Irving knew how to set a scene. He did this by adopting the presumed style of his imaginary author, Diedrich Knickerbocker, and it is impossible not to quote at least several paragraphs from his delightful pseudo-*History:*

"The ship in which these illustrious adventurers set sail was called the Goede Vrouw, or good woman, in compliment to the wife of the President of the West India Company, who was allowed by every body (except her husband) to be a sweet-tempered lady—when not in liquor. It was in truth a most gallant vessel, of the most approved Dutch construction, and made by the ablest ship-carpenters of Amsterdam, who, it is well known, always model their ships after the fair forms of their countrywomen. Accordingly, it had one hundred feet in the beam, one hundred feet in the keel, and one hundred feet from the bottom of the stern-post to the tafferel. Like the beauteous model, who was declared to be the greatest belle in Amsterdam, it was full in the bows, with a pair of enormous cat-heads, a copper bottom, and withal a most prodigious poop!

"The architect, who was somewhat of a religious man, far from decorating the ship with pagan idols, such as Jupiter, Neptune, or Hercules, (which heathenish abominations, I have no doubt occasion the misfortunes and shipwreck of many a noble vessel,) he, I say, on the contrary, did laudably erect for a head, a goodly image of St. Nicholas, equipped with a low, broad-brimmed hat, huge pair of Flemish trunk hose, and a pipe that reached to the end of the bowsprit. Thus gallantly furnished, the stanch ship floated sideways, like a majestic goose, out of the harbor of the great city of Amsterdam, and all the bells, that were not otherwise engaged, rang a triple bobmajor on the joyful occasion."

The Knickerbocker *History* makes much of the influence and revelatory dreaming of one Oloffe Van Kortlandt, who served on the Dutch development council for the new territory. But Van Kortlandt claimed that "the good St. Nicholas had appeared to him in a dream the night before" and urged that they consider a proper site. Van Kortlandt said that he had recognized the saint "by his broad hat, his long pipe and the resemblance which he bore to the figure on the bow of the *Goede Vrouw.*" Irving, alias Knickerbocker, writes that "many have thought this dream was a mere invention of Oloffe Van Kortlandt; who, it is said, had ever regarded [the competing real estate area of] Communipaw with an evil eye because he had arrived there after all the land had been shared out, and who was anxious to change the seat of the empire to some new place, where he might be present at the distribution of new lots."

Elsewhere in the book he describes how this selfsame Oloffe had dropped off to sleep after a particularly ample meal, and he continues:

"And the sage Oloffe dreamed a dream—and lo, the good St. Nicholas came riding over the tops of the trees, in that selfsame wagon wherein he brings his yearly presents to children, and he descended hard by where the heroes of Communipaw had made their late repast. And he lit his pipe by the fire, and sat himself down and smoked; and as he smoked the smoke from his pipe ascended into the air and spread like a cloud overhead. And Oloffe bethought him, and he hastened and climbed up to the top of one of the tallest trees, and saw that the smoke spread over a great extent of country—and as he considered it more attentively, he fancied that the great volume of smoke assumed a variety of marvelous forms, where in dim obscurity he saw shadowed out palaces and domes and lofty spires, all of which lasted but a moment, and then faded away, until the whole rolled off, and nothing but the green woods were left. And when St. Nicholas had smoked his pipe, he twisted it in his hat-band, and laying his finger beside his nose, gave the astonished Van Kortlandt a very significant look, then mounting his wagon, he returned over the tree-tops and disappeared.

"And Van Kortlandt awoke from his sleep greatly instructed, and he aroused his companions, and related to them his dream, and interpreted it, that it was the will of St. Nicholas that they should settle down and build the city here. And that the smoke of the pipe was a type how vast would be the extent of the city; inasmuch as the volumes of its smoke would spread over a wide extent of country. And they all with one voice assented to this interpretation excepting Mynheer Ten Broeck, who declared the meaning to be that it would be a city wherein a little fire would occasion a great smoke, or in other words, a very vaporing little city—both which interpretations have strangely come to pass!

"The great object of their perilous expedition, therefore, being thus happily accomplished, the voyagers returned merrily to Communipaw, where they were received with great rejoicings. And here calling a general meeting of all the wise men and the dignitaries of Pavonia, they related the whole history of their voyage, and of the dream of Oloffe Van Kortlandt. And the people lifted up their voices and blessed the good St. Nicholas, and from that time forth the sage Van Kortlandt was held in more honor than ever, for his great talent at dreaming, and was pronounced a most useful citizen and a right good man—when he was asleep."

Irving's polished satire is evident in his account of the purchase of Manhattan from the Indians for a few beads and trinkets, as he writes: "The land being thus fair purchased, of the Indians, a circumstance very unusual in the history of colonization, and strongly illustrative of the honesty of our Dutch progenitors, a stockade, fort and trading house were forthwith erected on an eminence in front of the place where the good St. Nicholas had appeared in a vision to Oloffe the Dreamer; and which, as has been observed, was the identical place at present known as Bowling Green." New Yorkers know Bowling Green as the tiny park close to the southern end of Manhattan, where the skyscrapers of Wall Street meet the Atlantic Ocean.

The metamorphosis of Saint Nicholas, the forbidding tall figure who appeared in icons, sculptures, paintings, and stained-glass windows, to the roly-poly Santa Claus of today, was achieved by the same team of Irving, Moore, and Nast. Raymond Schuessler, writing on the question "How Santa Claus Grew Fat" in *American Heritage* (Winter 1952), notes that he "has not always been the overfed rascal that he is today" and had previously been imagined "literally thin enough to get down the chimney." But Moore in his verse, "taking a cue from Washington Irving's literary conception," portrays Santa as roly-poly, broad-faced with merry dimples, twinkling eyes and cheeks "like roses."

"Nowadays," Schuessler writes, "to picture Santa as anything but huge, pink and exuberant would start a major uprising.

. . . The history of the popular idealization of St. Nicholas is strange but not inexplicable," as Santa's changing appearance through the years "has come about through a combination of artistic progress and more universal acceptance of Santa Claus as the vivacious personification of Christmas cheer; after all an emaciated Santa would hardly appear healthy, much less jocose." Schuessler notes that the saint remained "consistently tall and thin in the public print until the 1860's when a cartoonist of the period, Thomas Nast, began drawing Santa Claus for book illustrations which closely resembled Moore's written description."

The trio of Irving, Moore, and Nast fixed the details of Santa's image which we now regard as age-old traditions. Schuessler reminds us that Nast's drawings established the popular notion of Santa that led to the present-day conception. He notes that Nast "popularized not only the figure of Santa Claus but also many of the other practices with which he is associated at Christmas: building the toys in his North Pole workshops, keeping the records of good and bad children, receiving and answering their letters and driving his reindeer." Today, if you should come across a picture of Santa and his reindeer in a local Lapland newspaper, right in the heart of reindeer country, remember: it all started in New York. Thomas Nast St. Hill, the artist's grandson, says in his book *Thomas Nast's Christmas Drawings* that his grandfather's sketches marked "the first appearance of Santa Claus as we know him today." He says that Moore, "the learned American professor, and Thomas Nast, the young German-born artist, gave the world a new image of St. Nicholas and one that would live in the hearts of children for generations to come." But, he adds, had Nast not brought Moore's "jolly old elf" to life in his drawings, "the St. Nicholas described by Moore's pen might never have survived." Other artists embellished the figure, often in advertisements, and department stores throughout the country made the Santa Claus figure the center of their Christmas promotions.

Here, then, is the full text of Clement Clarke Moore's "A Visit from St. Nicholas," as he originally wrote it for his children:

'Twas the night before Christmas when all through the house
Not a creature was stirring, not even a mouse;
The stockings were hung by the chimney with care,
In hopes that St. Nicholas soon would be there;
The children were nestled all snug in their beds,
While visions of sugar-plums danced through their heads;
And Mamma in her kerchief, and I in my cap,
Had just settled our brains for a long winter's nap—
When out on the lawn there rose such a clatter,
I sprang from my bed to see what was the matter.
Away to the window I flew like a flash.
Tore open the shutters and threw up the sash.
The moon, on the breast of the new-fallen snow,
Gave a luster of mid-day to objects below,
When, what to my wondering eyes should appear
But a miniature sleigh, and eight tiny reindeer,
With a little old driver, so lively and quick,
I knew in a moment it must be St. Nick.

More rapid than eagles his coursers they came,
And he whistled, and shouted, and called them by name;
"Now, Dasher! now, Dancer! now, Prancer and Vixen!
On, Comet! on, Cupid! on, Dunder and Blitzen—
To the top of the porch, to the top of the wall!
Now, dash away, dash away, dash away all!"
As leaves that before the wild hurricane fly,
When they meet with an obstacle, mount to the sky,
So, up to the house top the coursers they flew,
With a sleigh full of toys—and St. Nicholas, too.

And then in a twinkling I heard on the roof,
The prancing and pawing of each little hoof.
As I drew in my head, and was turning around,
Down the chimney St. Nicholas came with a bound.
He was dressed all in fur from his head to his foot,
And his clothes were all tarnished with ashes and soot;
A bundle of toys he had flung on his back.
And he looked like a peddler just opening his pack.
His eyes how they twinkled! his dimples how merry!
His cheeks were like roses, his nose like a cherry;
His droll little mouth was drawn up like a bow,
And the beard on his chin was as white as the snow.
The stump of a pipe he held tight in his teeth,
And the smoke, it encircled his head like a wreath.

He had a broad face, and a little round belly,
That shook when he laughed, like a bowl full of jelly.
He was chubby and plump—a right jolly old elf;
And I laughed when I saw him, in spite of myself.
A wink of his eye, and a twist of his head,
Soon gave me to know I had nothing to dread.
He spoke not a word, but went straight to his work,
And filled all the stockings; then turned with a jerk,
And laying his finger aside of his nose,
And giving a nod, up the chimney he rose.
He sprang to his sleigh, to his team gave a whistle,
And away they all flew like the down of a thistle;
But I heard him exclaim, ere he drove out of sight,
"HAPPY CHRISTMAS TO ALL
AND TO ALL A GOOD NIGHT!"

Dr. Clement Clarke Moore, whose poem "A Visit from St. Nicholas" decisively changed the image of the saint in the United States and most of Western culture, gave a first reading of it to his children on December 23, 1822. Yet, it might never have reached beyond the Moore home if it had not delighted a lady visitor, daughter of the Reverend David Butler. She copied the poem and had it published the following year in the *Sentinel* of Troy, New York. From there, in reprints and anthologies, its words entered the language: " 'Twas the night before Christmas," "visions of sugar-plums," "Now, Dasher! now, Dancer! now, Prancer and Vixen!" and "a sleigh full of toys," "a bundle of toys he had flung on his back," "a right jolly old elf" who "filled all the stockings" and "up the chimney he rose" to enter "his sleigh."

Actually, Dr. Moore kept his authorship of the poem a secret for many years. But when he published an anthology of his verse in 1844, he included "A Visit from St. Nicholas" in the volume bearing his name. To the degree that the images used in the poem reflected earlier European folkloric elements, they had been echoed, sifted, and transformed by Moore's imagination. Santa's fur costume can be traced to such regional traditions as that of the Pelz-Nicol in southern Germany, or the gnomelike tradition of the Jul-Nissen in Scandinavia. In Sweden, specifically, the Jul-Tomten is a gnomelike figure; children's books have tended to make the tomten into a troll who lives in the woods with his family and appears at Christmastime to bring presents.

In Sweden, too, one origin of the reindeer image used by Moore may be found in the tradition that the Jul-Bocken, or Christmas Buck, is a carrier of Christmas presents. But cultural crossfertilization, in which the Irving-Moore-Nast version of the "American" Santa Claus proved the strongest strain, has made a present-giving Santa figure popular in Sweden as well.

The names of the reindeer in the Moore mythology are a mixed bunch. Donner and Blitzen are clearly German, from Thunder *(Donner)* and Lightning *(Blitz);* Moore probably just liked the sound of these two onomatopoetic words. Dasher is, of course, a dashing animal; Prancer is prancing in the best manner of a show horse; and Dancer needs no explanation whatever. Vixen is the word for a female fox, Comet and Cupid can be interpreted any way one likes. Moore probably just liked the rhythm and alliteration of these names.

Two years before Dr. Moore read his poem to his children, Washington Irving published his *Sketch Book*, which contains a lively description of an old Yorkshire country house at Christmas, with carol singing, yule log, mingling of the masters and servants, holly, ivy, and mistletoe. Irving's description was prompted by the author's visit to Bracegirdle Hall, Yorkshire, in 1820. He was taken to the village by Sir Walter Scott, who had been delighted with "Diedrich Knickerbocker's" *History* of New York.

Publishers, writers, and illustrators have played a crucial role in the evolution of Saint Nicholas into Santa Claus. *Harper's Weekly* not only printed many of Thomas Nast's drawings of Santa but also numerous poems and texts by others that helped shape the image during the nineteenth century. Nast's drawings of Santa Claus tended to reflect the artist's boyhood memories of Bavaria (geographically adjacent to Austria, which gave us the song "Silent Night" and other associations with the Christmas tree).

Despite all its admixtures of European symbols and memories, today's Santa Claus figure is clearly the creation of nineteenth-century America.

Saint Nicholas, as sculpted in an old Dutch cookie. *Collection of Dr. Joost A. M. Meerloo, Amsterdam*

This tablet, on display in Amsterdam, pictures "Sinter Claes" as the city's patron saint, while showing him in the act of restoring the three students to life.

Nineteenth-century woodcut of Saint Nicholas of Myra, by an anonymous Greek artist.

"Seeing Santa Claus," by Thomas Nast. From *Harper's Weekly*, January 1, 1876.

Washington Irving (1783–1859). Pen and wash drawing by John Wesley Jarvis, 1809. *Yale University Art Gallery*

Clement Clarke Moore (1779–1863), as painted by Daniel Huntington. Courtesy of General Theological Seminary, New York, N.Y. *Frick Art Reference Library*

Thomas Nast (1840–1902). Self-sketch.

"A Visit from Saint Nicholas," Thomas Nast's first published Santa Claus picture. From *Christmas Poems,* 1863–64.

Old SANTECLAUS with much delight

His reindeer drives this frosty night,

O'er chimney tops, and tracks of snow,

To bring his yearly gifts to you.

Before Santa Claus was shown with a team of reindeer, he had only one. This drawing, showing him driving over rooftops against a background of chimneys and a weathervane, appeared in *The Children's Friend: A New Year's Present to the Little Ones from Five to Twelve*, published in New York in 1821. *American Antiquarian Society, Worcester, Mass.*

Since the beginning of the century, newspapers and magazines each Christmas reprint the puzzled question of a very little girl, "Please tell me the truth, is there a Santa Claus?" And with it they publish the reply written by a gruff turn-of-the-century newspaperman, which contains the reassuring exclamation, "Yes, Virginia, there is a Santa Claus!"

This exchange has become part of contemporary American folklore. It fits into the mood of today's Christmas celebrations, its doubts, and a continuing need for reassurance. But how did it begin? Who was the questioning little girl, and who was the man who answered her?

At the time she put her question, Virginia O'Hanlon was eight years old and lived with her parents at 115 West 95th Street in New York City. She was the daughter of Dr. Philip F. O'Hanlon, a consulting surgeon of the Police Department. She later recalled that, being an only child, her parents "did everything for me that any parents could do." She believed in Santa Claus "quite naturally," as he had "never disappointed" her; but when other little boys and girls told her that there really wasn't any Santa Claus, she was "filled with doubts" and found her father "a little evasive on the subject." As she told the story to a group of Hunter students, this is what followed:

"It was a habit in our family that whenever any doubts came up as to how to pronounce a word, or some question of historical fact was in doubt, we wrote to the 'Question and Answer' column in the *Sun* [then a daily paper in New York]. Father would always say, 'If you see it in the *Sun* it's so,' and that settled the matter.

" 'Well, I'm just going to write to the *Sun*, and find out the real truth,' I said to father.

"He said, 'Go ahead, Virginia. I'm sure the *Sun* will give you the right answer, as it always does.' "

The little girl's letter, addressed, "Dear Editor," and giving her age, said:

"Some of my little friends say there is no Santa Claus. Papa says 'If you see it in the *Sun* it's so.' Please tell me the truth, is there a Santa Claus?"

She signed the letter with her full name, added the O'Hanlon address, mailed it off to the paper, and began looking every day for a reply in the Question and Answer column. Virginia became more and more disappointed. No reply appeared, and she felt that "the editor had not thought my letter important enough to answer."

But one day Dr. O'Hanlon called his daughter from his downtown office and told her, "Virginia, they did answer your letter. They gave you a whole editorial."

The *Sun* editorial, entitled "Yes, Virginia, there is a Santa Claus!" appeared on September 21, 1897. It began by saying, "We take pleasure in answering at once and thus prominently the communication below, expressing at the same time our great satisfaction that its faithful author is numbered among the friends of the *Sun.*" After giving the text of the girl's letter, the editorial continued:

"Virginia, your little friends are wrong. They have been affected by the skepticism of a skeptical age. They do not believe except they see. They think that nothing can be which is not comprehensible by their little minds.

"All minds, Virginia, whether they be men's or children's, are little. In this great universe of ours man is a mere insect, an ant, in his intellect, as compared with the boundless world about him, as measured by the intelligence capable of grasping the whole of truth and knowledge.

"Yes, Virginia, there is a Santa Claus. He exists as certainly as love and generosity and devotion exist, and you know that they abound and give to your life its highest beauty and joy. Alas! How dreary would be the world if there were no Santa Claus! It would be as dreary as if there were no Virginias.

"There would be no childlike faith then, no poetry, no romance to make tolerable this existence. We should have no enjoyment except in sense and sight. The eternal light with which childhood fills the world would be extinguished.

"Not believe in Santa Claus! You might as well not believe in fairies! You might get your papa to hire men to watch in all the Chimneys on Christmas Eve to catch Santa Claus, but even if they did not see Santa Claus coming down, what would that prove?

"Nobody sees Santa Claus, but that is no sign that there is no Santa Claus. The most real things in the world are those that neither children nor men can see. Did you ever see fairies dancing on the lawn? Of course not, but that's no proof that they are not there. Nobody can conceive or imagine all the wonders there are unseen and unseeable in the world.

"You tear apart a baby's rattle and see what makes the noise inside, but there is a veil covering the unseen world which not the strongest man, nor even the united strength of all the strongest men that ever lived, could tear apart.

"Only faith, fancy, poetry, love, romance, can push aside that curtain and view and picture the supernatural beauty and glory beyond. Is it all real? Ah, Virginia, in all this world there is nothing else real and abiding.

"No Santa Claus! Thank God he lives, and he lives forever. A thousand years from now, Virginia, nay, ten times ten thousand years from now, he will continue to make glad the heart of childhood."

This affirmation of the power of "love and generosity and devotion" was written by Francis Pharcellus Church. Later his colleagues said that he had not at first cherished the editorial assignment which was forwarded to him by the Question and Answer department of the newspaper. The *New York Times,* for whom he had served as Civil War correspondent before joining the *Sun* as an editorial writer, noted (May 14, 1971) that Church, the son of a Baptist minister, was "a man of sardonic bent whose personal motto was, 'Endeavor to clear you mind of cant.' "

The *Times* also said: "Virtually unknown by name outside his own personal and professional circles," Mr. Church specialized in writing editorials on controversial theological subjects. He had been on the staff of the *Sun* for about 20 years when the assignment to answer Virginia's letter came to him."

The *Times* also recalled that "the editorial was reprinted annually before Christmas in the staid columns of the *Sun,* but until he died, married but childless, nine years later on April 11, 1906, it was not generally known that Mr. Church was the author." In fact, the *Times* admitted that, in its own obituary of Francis Church and in an editorial that followed, the paper "did not mention Virginia's letter and Mr. Church's reply." The letter last appeared in the *Sun* in 1949. Ten days after Christmas, on January 4, 1950, the paper ceased publication; it merged with the *New York World-Telegram,* which kept the words *and Sun* in its masthead.

In its obituary on Mrs. Laura Virginia O'Hanlon Douglas,

published May 14, 1971, the *New York Times* made up for its earlier omissions. It observed that Mr. Church's famous words became "one of the best-known editorials in American journalism," later "spread around the world in countless reprintings, in newspapers and anthologies, and in translations into some 20 languages."

Mrs. O'Hanlon Douglas died in Valatie, New York, on May 13, 1971, at the age of eighty-one. Murray Ilson, in the *Times*'s obituary, said that "no editorial was more famous" than that inspired by Virginia's letter. She received a Bachelor of Arts degree from Hunter College, New York, in 1910 and a Master's Degree from Columbia University the following year. In 1912 she became a teacher in the New York City school system.

While working as a grade-school teacher, Virginia O'Hanlon studied for her doctorate, which she received from Fordham University. She became a junior principal in 1935. The obituary noted that "for three years before she retired, Mrs. Douglas, by then a widow, had been junior principal of Public School 401 in Brooklyn, which holds classes in hospitals and institutions where children are chronically ill."

Virginia O'Hanlon Douglas spent a total of forty-seven years in the New York school system. At the age of forty-four she revisited her alma mater, Hunter College, and told students that the newspaper's reply to her childhood inquiry had been the outstanding event in her life. Shortly before her retirement she reflected on this event, and on her involvement with children, their hopes and ideas. She said that children were "naturally so sincere and so serious about things that you feel you wouldn't want to disappoint them." Thus, the reassurance she had received as a girl of eight became, in the elaboration of her work as a teacher, a basic theme of her career.

The New York School of Printing reproduced the *Sun*'s Santa Claus editorial for Mrs. Douglas's private use as a handsomely printed sheet. She used the sheet to answer requests for text, which continued throughout her life. It was a message which, in many and more sophisticated ways, she communicated to the thousands of children who were her pupils during nearly half a century of teaching, as she thought to "make glad the heart of childhood."

The familiar rotund figure of Santa Claus, which succeeded the more gnomelike image developed by Thomas Nast, emerged from a series of paintings—begun in the 1920's—by Haddon Sundblom for The Coca-Cola Company. Together with the Santa figure which was annually televised from the parade organized by R. H. Macy, the New York department store, Mr. Sundblom's elaboration of the Santa Claus figure achieved firm status among children and adults alike. The painting reproduced here, which originally appeared in an advertisement, uses such symbols as a ledger containing entries on "Good Boys and Girls" and a globe indicating Santa's worldwide travels. *The Coca-Cola Company, Atlanta, Georgia*

10. A PILGRIMAGE TO MYRA

This interior photograph of the Church of Saint Nicholas at Demre (Myra) shows the semicircular seating arrangement, resembling a miniature stadium, with remnants of an altar, flanked by four pillars in the center.

You can go to the birthplace of Saint Nicholas, Patara, or to Myra (now called Demre). Both are off the beaten tourist paths. To visit these sites in the twentieth century, you first take a plane to Istanbul. From there, boats of the Turkish Maritime Lines make regularly scheduled trips to southwestern Turkey. The *S.S. Samsun*, for instance, leaves Istanbul on Thursdays and arrives at the small port of Finike the following Sunday. From there, you can take a bus to Demre. The distance is a little over twenty miles. Or, you can go by air to the larger city, Antalya, whose Archeological Museum contains building remnants of the Church of Saint Nicholas at Demre (Myra), as well as relics of the saint. A soft surface road, from Antalya to Demre, accommodates cars and buses.

To go to Patara, the saint's birthplace, you take a boat to Fetiye. From there, a bus passes through the wooded countryside of eucalyptus trees. After a few hours, it stops by a weather-beaten sign that says "Patara." The path to the village from the road leads through fields by the Xanthus River, passing a Roman archway. Hidden off the path is a granary built by Emperor Hadrian; other Roman ruins are prominent, among them a large theater whose lower section is submerged in sand while the upper rows offer a view of the Mediterranean Sea.

You travel another fifty miles east of Patara to reach Demre. On the way, you pass through the somewhat larger village of Kas. The road to Demre follows the mountainside and stays close to the Mediterranean Sea. Roman and Greek ruins are visible here and there. Most of the traffic consists of loaded donkeys, and there are a few camels. Groves of olive trees, the eternal vegetation of the Near East, dominate the sun-drenched countryside.

Demre is a tiny village. Time here has not quite stood still, but it seems at least a half-century or a century behind bustling Istanbul. You can stop on the village square for a bowl of yogurt, some cheese and olives, or apricots from the local orchards. The countryside is fertile. Rich soil, deposited by overflowing waters, have raised the level of the land so that the Church of Saint Nicholas is now considerably below the road and the adjacent farms.

As you look down from the high ground, the church seems small and forlorn. Part of the roof is covered with tin. A bell tower, obviously a fairly recent addition, rises above the building in three levels that form two balconies. When the sun hits the tower, it stands out against the evening shade on the hills in the background. The southern end of the church features a court with columns that have tops of Corinthian design.

Inside the church, within a side aisle, stands what is claimed to be the empty tomb of Saint Nicholas. The villagers of Demre say that a hole in the side of the tomb shows where the saint's relics were removed by sailors from Bari. It is a church that could have accommodated only a small congregation; ten rows of seats form a semicircle. The interior is bare. You can view building fragments, and bits of pottery that either actually or symbolically represent the period of the Bishop of Myra's presence in the village. A ship's bell is also on display, illustrating Saint Nicholas's traditional role as the patron of sailors.

Once you have scrambled back up to the road's level, with its hot dust and clean air, you may wonder whether the whitewashed, empty church is itself a mere relic of a bygone era, or whether the spirit of Saint Nicholas does somehow remain. Your feelings depend, of course, more on your own state of mind than on the rough charm of the little ecclesiastical building. Chances are that the actual tomb of Saint Nicholas could not have stood the ravages of time and that the Early Roman craftsmanship of this sarcophagus marks it as a later substitute for the real burial place of the saint.

The Near East, cradle of our civilization, has seen a wide-ranging and often violent succession of cultures and faiths. Empires have succeeded one another, have expanded and contracted; religions, languages, and modes of living have intermingled, fed on one another, crushed one another. The Greco-Roman periods that left their marks on Myra were superseded by Turkic-Islamic culture. The little church in Demre is an isolated remnant; the spirit of Saint Nicholas is alive, but quite elusive in this sleepy Turkish village, whose shepherds share the afternoon sun with their grazing flocks, whose rich orchards are filled with the vitality of nature, brimming with greens and reds, in leaf and fruit—while encroaching from higher ground on the crumbling stones of the little church below.

The spirit of Saint Nicholas traveled north toward Kiev and all of Russia, west toward Bari and Western Europe. From the United States, much transformed, it spread across the world. But can it be found today in Demre? Only if you bring it with you, determined to recapture a distant past. A pilgrimage to the one-time village of Myra is a journey into yourself. You, the visitor, are the carrier of Saint Nicholas's symbolism, whatever you perceive it to be.

There is a very slight possibility—chances are a thousand to one—that the Bishop of Myra never even existed, that not only his miraculous achievements are pious legends but that there never was a Nicholas, born in Patara, who attained the rank of bishop in the town of Myra. When you turn to the superskeptical historians, you discover that his name has not been found in all the listings of those who attended the First Council at Nicaea.

And yet: Does the "historical" Saint Nicholas of Myra and Bari really matter? It does not in the human and therefore ultimate sense. Saint Nicholas as a symbol of assurance, trust, piety, kindness, and selflessness is far more important than any missing element of historical documentation. We share with those who first admired, then embellished, and eventually worshiped the Saint Nicholas personality, a need to personalize our emotions. If something is deeply desired but cannot be seen or touched or heard, we have the ability to create it. We envision, we hallucinate, we shape in humble or sophisticated artistry what we lack. When Poseidon had been forgotten, when the Temple of Artemis was destroyed, the sailors who daily faced the unpredictable dangers of wind and sea needed a protector, and they found Saint Nicholas. When the sea was tamed, but voyaging students were in danger, Saint Nicholas appeared as their patron. The patron saint of unmarried maidens, of corn, of newborn babes, was in a special sense a "fertility symbol," but not exclusively and not consistently.

It is fitting that the saint finally emerged as the protector and benefactor of children. If, in a Midwestern American town, even the name Santa Claus becomes the more familiar "Sandy Claus," it is fitted into a specific time and place and lends a neighborly affection that overcomes any fear of the supernaturally remote. The reincarnation of Saint Nicholas as our Santa Claus—through the artistic creativity of Irving, Moore, and

Nast, is merely a continuation of a process that has been going on for well over a thousand years. The Saint Nicholas of the Byzantine sailors differed from the saint whose awe-inspiring figure is found in the churches of Greece and Russia; the Italian painters and French legend-writers adapted the image to their times and needs, just as much as the New Yorkers of the nineteenth century.

Who are we to assume that our fears and wishes differ in substance from those of the fourth, ninth, or twelfth centuries? Our technology and communications are different, but only because they make the figure in a department store parade ubiquitous through color television. That adults, vicariously, experience the thrills of receiving gifts through their children is hardly more than a brief revisiting of childhood itself. We never outgrow being children. In so-called "primitive" societies, this tendency is more openly expressed than in our own civilization, where *immature* is a word of denigration. One "primitive" culture, that of Polynesia as expressed clearly in New Guinea, retains such childlike expectations of gifts in our time. This is the so-called Cargo Cult, which in certain areas has had disastrous results.

Those who practice the Cargo Cult are usually following a persuasive leader who claims an inspiration that will lead to untold riches. If, he says, the communities will only make the appropriate sacrifices to the gods, vast "cargo"—gifts of all sorts, including a variety of modern gadgets—will descend on them. Over and over again, New Guinea tribes have consumed their produce and livestock in superfeasts (akin to the abundance of an American Christmas meal) in order to show their trust in the gods' ultimate generosity. Having observed the arrival of vast quantities of goods at airfields in western New Guinea, one tribe even built primitive replicas of ramps on land that had been cleared to make room for the landing of divine cargo.

This extreme manifestation of the desire to get something for nothing (or at least in exchange for the right words, the correct ritual) expresses a timeless, universal human hope. The gambler, the race-track habitué, and the buyer of lottery tickets act on similar hopes, beliefs, or delusions. But while the followers of the Cargo Cult are sure to be disappointed (their leader will tell them that their ritual was somehow imperfect), and while the overall odds are against him, the small child's belief in Santa

Claus will be rewarded. This earnest belief, this untainted faith, is based on an innocence that has not yet been wounded by the sharp edges of reality. It is proper, I think, that such innocence be respected. What, indeed, do we have to offer as a replacement for faith and trust? Only knowledge, with all its imperfections. If the spirit of Saint Nicholas lives in our time, it is not to be found during a pilgrimage to the sunken church in Myra (Demre), but among adults who are privileged to see a bright-eyed child discover a gift that Santa Claus has brought during the night.

Dr. Joost A.M. Meerloo, the Dutch-born psychoanalyst who practiced in the United States for many years before retiring to his homeland, recalls in a paper on "Santa Claus and the Psychology of Giving" that the annual "Sint Nicolaas" celebrations in his native country had a lasting impact on him: "Even when I now say that I no longer believe in the old bishop's existence, I realize that deep inside of me the same excitement I felt when I was a boy is aroused in me every year with the approach of the good Saint's birthday. The early festive conditioning and expectation is still there." Dr. Meerloo sees the Saint Nicholas cult, down to its manifestations in our day, as the celebration that responds to such deeply rooted, instinctual urges as the need to be given, the need to procreate, the battle between good and evil. During the celebrations, he notes, "socially banned aggressions can be expressed with good grace," and the ritual of mutual giving covers "the ambivalence of give-and-take beautifully."

Of the Saint Nicholas legend in general, Dr. Meerloo writes: "In the deepest sense, he bestows the gift of continual revival upon man, the blessing of children, which were the first reassurances and life investments of his ancestors. He directs the eternal battle between good and evil, and somehow during the long nights of the winter solstice, he gets into everybody's blood to arouse holy and worldly sentiments."

We are not, then, I suggest, betraying the Saint Nicholas tradition with our contemporary variations on the theme of gift-giving; we have merely adapted it to our civilization and its needs. In fact, by retaining the Santa Claus image and its implications of selfless giving, we are perpetuating an altruistic image of ourselves. We are, despite the pressures of a materialistic civilization, capable of giving for giving's sake. Dr. Bruno

Bettelheim, the child psychiatrist and professor of education at the University of Chicago, believes that children should not be robbed of their belief in Santa Claus too early because "benign fantasies" are a good thing in this "cruel world."

From the empty tomb in Myra, and the imposing Basilica in Bari, through the pen of Thomas Nast, we find the image and the message that urges us to regain our own innocence, at least now and then. I do not assume that we will experience a renaissance of Saint Nicholas-consciousness, apart from the Christmas season, throughout the year. And yet, this image and this spirit are capable of bringing out the best in us: the childlike joy, the selfless giving of gifts—and of ourselves—which Saint Nicholas has come to symbolize through the centuries.

Sarcophagus in the Church of Saint Nicholas at Demre (Myra), said to be the coffin which held the remains of the saint until it was broken into, during the eleventh century, when the saint's relics were removed to Bari.

Church of Saint Nicholas at Demre (Myra), showing excavated sections, with later additions—including tower—behind them. *Turkish Information Office*

SELECTED BIBLIOGRAPHY

Anrich, Gustav. *Hagios Nikolaos*. Berlin-Leipzig, 1913–1917, Vols. I and II.

Butler's Lives of Saints. Edited, Revised and Supplemented by Herbert Thurston, S.J., and Donald Attwater. New York, 1963, Vol. IV.

Chambers, R. *The Book of Days II*. London, 1863.

Craddick, Ray A. "Size of Santa Claus Drawings as a Function of Time Before and After Christmas." *Journal of Psychological Studies*, Vol. XII, No. 3, 1961.

Crozier, Eric. *The Life and Legends of Saint Nicholas, Patron Saint of Children*. London, 1949.

De Groot, Andriaan D. *Saint Nicholas: A psychoanalytic study of his history and myth*. Amsterdam, 1969.

Jones, Charles W. "Knickerbocker Santa Claus." *New-York Historical Society Quarterly*, Vol. XXXVIII, No. 4.

McKnight, George H. *St. Nicholas: His Legend and His Role in the Christmas Celebration and Other Popular Customs*. New York, 1917.

Meisen, Karl. *Nikolauskult und Nikolausbrauch im Abendlande*. Düsseldorf, 1931.

Moran, Hugh A. *The Story of Santa Claus*. Palo Alto, 1952.

Nitti di Vitto, Franceso. *La Leggenda della traslazione di S. Nicola di Bari*. Bari, undated.

Patterson, Samuel White. *The Poet of Christmas Eve: A Life of Clement Clarke Moore, 1779–1863*. New York, 1956.

Ramsay, W. M. *The Historial Geography of Asia Minor*. Royal Geographical Society, London. Supplementary Papers IV, 1890.

Schuessler, Raymond. "How Santa Claus Grew Fat." *American Heritage*, Vol. III, No. 2, Winter 1952.

Sereno, Renzo. "Some Observations on the Santa Claus Custom." *Psychiatry*, Vol. XIV, No. 4, November 1951.

Simons, Gerald. *Barbarian Europe*. Washington, D.C., 1968.

SANTA CLAUS.

MERRY CHRISTMAS

WITHDRAWN

DATE DUE			
AUG 27 '79			
JAN 2 '80			